ALL
IN
THE
NAME
OF
LOVE

Barbara and Glenn Smyly

Alivening Publications
P.O. Box 1368
Land O'Lakes, Florida 33539

Library of Congress Cataloging-in-Publication Data

Smyly, Glenn, 1942 - ∞
  All in the Name of Love

  Bibliography: p.
  1. Self-confidence. 2. Love. 3. Conduct of life.
I. Smyly, Barbara, 1956 - ∞   . II. Title.
BJ1533.S27S69 1986   131   86-14090
ISBN 0-9616707-0-3
ISBN 0-9616707-1-1 (pbk.)

Portions reprinted by permission from *A Course in Miracles,* © Copyright 1975, Foundation for Inner Peace, Inc.

ISBN 0-9616707-0-3

10 9 8 7 6 5 4 3 2

To our parents :

Joan Clark
Lawrence Dolan
Evelyn Wendt
Carlton Smyly

With love and deep appreciation.

ACKNOWLEDGMENTS

There are a number of people we want to acknowledge for their contribution to our success in this work for these past years.

We would like to start by thanking all those who have participated in the Alivening Weekends, the One Year Seminars, The Week Long Programs in Florida, The Support Teams, The Facilitators Program, The Set Up Teams, The Leadership Program participants and all other activities we have led.

Our thanks also to all those who invited their friends, families, and loved ones to participate with us in these events. Without you we would not have been able to do the work that we have done.

There were many who opened their homes for us to have the Weekends and One Year Seminars. We are grateful for their willingness to support Alivening so selflessly and for their commitment to bring their friends, family and loved ones more alive. We thank all of you. Your contribution to us is priceless and the difference you have made is immeasurable.

We also thank those who read, edited, and contributed to the final form of this book. They are Bill Mingen, Phil Laut, Buddy Sears, Sonya Whynman, Al and Deanna Carmen, and Craig Desha.

We also wish to thank Barbara and Robert Varley, Stan and Donna Fisher Tyler for their "dessert cards," the *Excerpts from A Course in Miracles*. There is a dessert card at the end of each chapter, each with a page reference to *A Course in Miracles*. The page reference "W,38" means "page 38 of the *Workbook*," and "T,216" means "page 216 of the *Textbook*."

There are some true national heroes that deserve our acknowledgement for their commitment to making our world a better place to live. They are: Jose Silva, for Silva Mind Control; Ken Keyes, for Living Love Courses, Books, and Tapes; Leonard Orr, for Rebirthing Sessions, Books, and Tapes; Helen Schucman, William Thetford, Robert Skutch, Judith Skutch, and the Foundation for Inner Peace, for *A Course in Miracles*; Werner Erhard for the Training and his Network of other related programs; Sai Baba, Babaji, and all those who have supported these people in presenting their work in the world.

Those who have contributed to this book are deeply appreciated. They have been an inspiration and a tremendous support. They are: Michelle Porcella, for Cover Design and Illustration; Theresa Plumley, for Typing; Tom Schunior Plum, for Typesetting and Consultation; Joan Hall, for Editing and Sourcing; Buddy Sears, for his Foreword and his support; Nikki Artale and Carol Kotopoulis for their continuing support; Phil Laut, for selling our book before it was even written; and Bert Field for the jacket text. Our thanks also to Linda Deutsch for entertaining us at all the right times.

We deeply thank our parents, Joan and Vinel Clark, Lawrence Dolan, Evelyn and Ray Wendt, and Carlton Smyly for teaching us patience, persistence, kindness, and for always assuring us that we can do *anything* we put our minds and hearts to. Their love and devotion is deeply and humbly appreciated.

Our special thanks to Joan Hall, Tom Plum, Caryn Clemons, Theresa Plumley, and Patricia Dolan for their love and support during the final days of editing this book. To say we could not have done it without them is an understatement. We could not have asked for dearer, more patient friends. We are forever grateful for their contribution to this book.

We appreciate and are grateful for our connection with our Father/Mother God for guiding and directing us in bringing forth this work and the opportunity to share it with you. May it truly make a difference in your life as you read and study it. Thank You!

CONTENTS

FOREWORD

In one breath, in one space, in one instant of time, you shall come to know yourself so fully that Heaven and Earth shall come together within you. You will know Love so completely that eternity shall unfold before you. You will arrive at the doorstep of immortality and the doors shall open unto your word . . . in one Breath, and this breath stretches across these pages into the pages of your heart, which shall read forever:

I AM THAT I AM: FULLY ALIVE AND COMPLETELY IN LOVE!!!!!

Barbara and Glenn have indeed contributed and surrendered their lives so very lovingly to bringing forth the Aliveness of all the spiritual teachers on the planet, to the awakening of Love deep within us, to be the powerful Beings God intended us to be.

That this book has come into your Life is no accident. It is, in fact, a sign of your awakening at hand. Not to be taken lightly, but taken to lighten the heart, this is your Manual to Aliveness, your map to Immortality, your very special gift from Barbara and Glenn.

Buddy Sears
Author of *Purpose: A Little Gift in the Adventure of Life*

1

CHAPTER 1

INTRODUCTION

This book is a result of twelve years of active participation on our part in almost every event available, to discover the truth about love. We have been to workshops, seminars, courses, colleges, gurus, masters and other teachers. We have read libraries of books and magazine articles, all to uncover the mystery of love. We have never believed that what we expressed as love and the way in which we acted was consistent with our experience of being in love. So our search began: to discover why love was expressed in such negative ways as war (fighting for the love of our country), divorce (loving enough to leave), child abuse (this hurts me more than it does you), spouse abuse (keeping her in line so she will not leave me), rape, incest, hate, etc.

The result of our searching was the development of our own program called the Alivening Weekend, which we have been leading for five years. We named it the Alivening Weekend because we noticed that people who do not express themselves and their love in positive ways are virtually not alive. This is so because all that people want is to be loved and to share their love with others, though not everyone acknowledges this.

In the Weekend, we gather together twenty people who are committed to discovering the truth about the way they have misused the power of love. The purpose of the Weekend is to heal their relationship with themeselves, to discover what love really is and to live from their hearts .. . to become Alive again. The results in their lives have been so dramatic that the participants have wanted all their loved ones to fall in love with themselves also, possibly for the first time. Since the Weekends are limited to only twenty people at a time and there are so many people on the same search, we asked God what to do about distributing these ideas to as many people as are interested as quickly as possible. Thus, this book.

The purpose of this book is for us to share with you what we have discovered from working with thousands of people in a very intimate way. We have the conviction that you will use this material. Use it to fall in love with yourself and others and to live life to its fullest from your heart, thus demonstrating your divinity and feeling more alive. This book is about the power of your word, your emotions and your connection to God.

Right from the beginning, it is important to make a distinction, or point out the differences, between listening and hearing, since most people believe them to be the same. Hearing is a physiological function of the ears that anyone who has the parts can do. Listening is a function of the heart. When you open your heart to listen to something, your whole body, mind and soul is engaged in the experience. This gives you the ability to integrate and assimilate the material listened to immediately. We can hear things over and over again and never listen to them or use them until such time as it becomes imperative for us to listen. How many times have we heard, "You never listen to me" from people who love us? Perhaps it is true; perhaps we are not listening. Hearing a train whistle does not effect us unless we are on the train tracks when we hear it. It then becomes imperative for us to listen.

Perhaps much of the material in this book you have heard before and never listened to. Now is the time to listen with your heart, mind and soul while you open yourself up to the message that is available to you. We ask that you make the distinction between listening and hearing while reading and integrating these words.

We all know that love is the only thing that will heal our planet and we are committed to doing all in our power to see love, peace and joy rule.

We invite you to enjoy the book, use it to its fullest potential, read it over and over again and fall in love with life.

As we have been working with people involving very sensitive areas of their lives, we are moved by the courage and trust they have demonstrated. They have opened themselves up completely and revealed their fears, hurts and doubts as well as their hopes, dreams and miracles. We do not take our relationship with them lightly. As such, we honor their confidentiality. It is in honor of our family of friends that we write this book.

The best way to get the maximum value from this book is to read it through. Then go back and read it doing all the recommended exercises.

We wish you Love, Happiness, Success, and Prosperity. Thank you for sharing our dream — your dream — this work.

Everything is for your
own best interest! W,38

CHAPTER 2

RESPONSIBILITY

In the beginning was the word. Most of us, throughout our lifetimes, have never been responsible for or questioned the word that we gave.

Let us talk about responsibility, since it is a widely used term in this book and in our world. Responsibility is not blame nor is it credit for the things that we have done. Responsibility, as used here, is simply the ownership of whatever has happened to us in our lives. Responsibility is the ultimate power when used appropriately. When you can be responsible for or take ownership of your life and affairs, you can be powerful in all areas of your life, regardless of the circumstances. Does this mean that you always know how or why you had your circumstances show up the way they did? No. It simply means, that when something happens that is upsetting or even exciting, that you look to yourself for the reasons or purpose rather than looking outside yourself for the cause of or solution to your situation.

Oftentimes, we look for someone or something to blame or credit the affairs of our life on — our boss, our spouse, our children, our parents, etc. In other words, it is our parents' fault that we do not make the kind of money we are worth because they did not put us through college or they did not give us the love we needed, etc. You can see how when you think others are responsible for your affairs that you are left powerless to change the situation. You are actually giving your power, by your word, to another; this leaves you helpless to change or resolve the situation.

One alternative is to be responsible for all of your life and affairs. We will tell you why.

When you take responsibility, *you* have the power to change the situation, *you* have the power to acknowledge your accomplishments for yourself and of yourself. When you hold others responsible for you, they have the power to change the situation. You are then left powerless in the situation, by your decree that they are responsible.

For instance, if you are not making the kind of money that you think you should be making, and you are responsible for that, you can begin to look at the attitudes you have about yourself that would keep you from attaining your goal of making more money. Maybe you have a low self esteem and do not feel you deserve it. Maybe you feel you are too young to make that kind of income. Maybe you just plain do not like your job and so you do not want to be promoted and thus be committed for another year, or whatever.

A problem with talking about responsibility is that most people have only used the word in the context that they are wrong or that they somehow did something wrong. Thus, people have a tendency to use responsibility to invalidate themselves. When used this way, one is also left powerless to change circumstances. The only way that we have any power to change our situation, is by being responsible for ourselves, our lives and our circumstances. We do that through giving our word that we are. If we would just keep telling ourselves that we are responsible for our lives, even when and especially when we do not want to be, or know that we cannot be, we would be more powerful, more peaceful and more trusting of ourselves.

Any and all situations can be changed or altered through giving our word that we are responsible and thus giving ourselves the power and permission to alter our circumstances. Our word is that powerful. OUR WORD IS THAT POWERFUL!

CHOICE

One of the most powerful responsibilities God gave man, which He/She gave no other of His/Her creatures on this planet is the power of choice. We have the ability to choose what we think, where we live, who we live with, under what conditions we will live, etc. Many people have never questioned their power to choose. Most take for granted their power and thus cannot or do not use it to problem solve or change their perception about certain situations. Nor do most people use it to change their ideals or to change their thoughts about themselves.

Choice means preference of one thing, idea or matter over another. When you are responsible you need to look at the choices you have made. So, if you did not go to college and you blamed it on your parents not having the money, the first choice you made was to have your parents pay for your college. Another choice you made in that situation was to only go to college on a full time basis; thus you also made the choice not to work or to work on a part time basis. As you carry this thought further to look for the various choices you made, for the most part unconsciously, you can see the many choices you made about NOT going to college. Given that we often make choices of this kind, we should not be surprised that we did not do what we said we wanted to do.

When we do not get what we want and we look to see what choices we have made in the matter, it becomes very clear that from the choices we made, we did in fact get what we asked for.

If our choices are to go to college full time and work only a few hours per week and we are in a family whose finances cannot support that choice, we are choosing not to go to college. We could have chosen to go to college part time and work part time. We could have chosen to get a student loan and go to college. We could have chosen any number of ways for us to go to college.

When we acknowledge that we are responsible, as in accountable for our lives, we have more of an opportunity to choose what we truly want in life. This is being responsible for your desires.

At the end of any upsetting time or a time when we did not acknowledge ourselves when we could have, we can look back and see what choices we made to bring about the situation we are in. This will fine tune our power to choose. Thus we can have some sense of mastery over choice the next time we are given the opportunity to choose. This is daily, by the way.

So far, we have spoken about choice and responsibility in our circumstances. Now, let us talk about our choices in our thoughts.

Humans have thousands of thoughts every day. We are totally unaware of most of them. Have you ever listened to what you are talking to yourself about? Try it. You will learn a lot about what you think about others and what you think about yourself. For the most part, we do not pay much attention to what we talk to ourselves about and we do not give much validity to the thoughts that we have.

What we choose then, is to be unconscious about our thoughts. Our thoughts are very powerful. We hear them over and over and over again daily, for years. Yet, we do not listen to most of them. We say, well it is just a thought. Our thoughts do produce results. This is why we can benefit from listening to what we are telling ourselves. Remember, our power lies in giving our word. Our thoughts are words and therefore call forth a result. We must start listening to what we are telling ourselves and choose to change our thoughts. The power in choice lies in what we are choosing to listen to. Let us change those thoughts which do not serve our highest good or call forth our desired and deserved good.

You may say that this is impossible to do. We have thousands of thoughts, how can we possibly catch every one? Perhaps we can not catch every one, but we can at least be committed to being vigilant with our minds.

Vigilance and persistence are what it takes to change the negative thoughts that we think about ourselves to the positive ones we choose to think. If whenever you have a negative thought — "They don't love me" — you cancel the thought and replace it with a positive thought — "Of course they love me" — eventually you will stop giving yourself what we call "cold pricklies." A cold prickly is anything negative that we say about ourselves or others.

So far we have trained our minds to think in a certain way. This has not always served us. Now is the time to choose what will replace the old worn out ways of thinking. We can choose love instead of hate. We can choose peace instead of war. We can choose harmony instead of discord. We choose whatever — instead of whatever. What we focus our thoughts on is what happens in our lives. The time has come to focus our thoughts on all the lovely, joyful things in life so that we can expand that joy throughout our world and make it a reality.

If we had an angel on our shoulder giving us everything that we thought and spoke, we would have to be very vigilant with what we thought or asked for. Wouldn't we? It is worth the vigilance. We are choosing by the power of our word what our life is.

All it takes is a commitment to yourself to be vigilant with your thoughts in order to expand choices in your life. The more vigilant you are with your thoughts, the more choices you will have. Consider, for a moment, that our minds are like an untrained St. Bernard dog. In order to train it we have to put a choke collar on it. Every time it starts to run away with us, we have to pull the collar and bring it back. So, every time your mind starts to run away with you, you can pull the collar and get back to what you choose to think.

We have all had something happen to demonstrate this. We know of a man who was terribly frightened of losing his wife. He loved her so much and could not imagine what life would be like without her. They worked together and very seldom were they apart. During one rare separation, he kept calling her and calling her until 4:00 in the morning and she was not home. He became more and more distraught and started imagining that she was out with other men, dancing, having a great time. The more he called and got no answer, the more angry and frustrated he became. She had never done anything to make him think that she would be unfaithful but after every phone call when she was not home yet, he would invent more stories about where she was and what she was doing. As you can imagine, by 4:00 a.m. he was terribly upset. He had a whole story made up in his mind about where she was, who she was with, how could she do this to him, he knew it would happen, etc. In the meantime, she arrived where he was staying at 4:15 a.m. to find him accusing her of the nastiest things. He did not even notice that she was there with him instead of in their home where he had been calling all night to find her. She had decided to fly to see him as a surprise because she missed him. She had been delayed in the airport for five hours and had just arrived. He was so convinced of the story he had built up over the five hours of waiting that it was hard for her to convince him otherwise. He finally remembered that she was supposed to be in another city that evening. Once he remembered, he could hear what had really happened.

He let his mind run away with him without pulling the collar.

For this couple, everything worked out humorously. For many, however, it does not. This is why we must be vigilant with our thoughts and be true to what we KNOW is real. It is very easy for us to convince ourselves that something is true when it is not.

This is why we must own the power of our choices. This man's choice to think the way he did about his wife affected not only his own peace of mind, but the rest of their family's peace as well.

By being responsible for the choices that we make, we can be free to make future choices.

Does this mean that the man was wrong for letting his imagination go? Not at all. In fact, he learned a great deal about his insecurities regarding his relationship and discovered what he really needed to be secure. He will never again, however, let his mind think those thoughts about his wife. He saw how deeply she was hurt by them. He now chooses to think positively about their relationship and the love they feel for each other.

So, choose thoughts that bring aliveness, joy, harmony and peace to your life. Your thoughts make a big difference in your world.

> *When you have accepted your mission*
> *to extend peace you will find peace,*
> *for by making it manifest you will*
> *be it!   T,216*

CHAPTER 3

THE POWER OF OUR WORD

In the past, many of the unconscious thoughts that we chose to believe were of hardship, loss, discord, etc.

Did you ever wonder why this is? Why would we choose to think of our world, our paradise in such a negative way?

Several research studies have been done in the last decade on life in utero. These studies have shown that early in a pregnancy, a child is able to respond to different sounds, emotions, and even in some cases commands. This new information has brought about quite a controversy in the field of psychology.

Many people are being regressed back to early childhood events, back to life in the womb, and in some cases back to their conception.

Those who have been regressed have found that early in childhood, at conception, at birth or in the womb, during a very upsetting time, they gave their word about how their life would be. We call this event a stand. In some cases before we were even born, we decided how life was going to be due to an upsetting time in the womb or at our conception. We stomped our foot, so to speak, and took a stand. Our word, mixed with the intensity of an upsetting emotion, about how the world was made this stand a reality.

We tell ourselves this stand over and over every day of our lives. We continually look for evidence in our daily affairs to make us right about what we said about how the world would be for us.

For many of us, birth was a very painful and terrifying experience. The pain of coming down the birth canal, the terror of being suffocated during this process, feeling gravity for the first time, feeling cold as we went from 105 degrees of water to 68 degrees of air, being laid on a cold scale, having our feet pricked, and a number of other things that happen at birth make our first impression of this world one of terror and horror. How could we *not* take a stand at this point, in such a situation. Most often, when people who have not taken a stand prior to birth reach this point of their delivery, a common stand taken is that they are not wanted, or loved. Whatever our stand, it derives additional power from the suppressed memory of birth. One of those memories is that "change leads to danger."

Life from there on is spent in search of love, while believing and proving to themselves that they are not loved. They will find spouses whom they perceive do not love them, children who will disrespect them, work that is unsatisfying, all to prove themselves right that they are not wanted or are not loved. If someone should come along who does truly love them they will perceive this person as weird or inauthentic, and will gather evidence to prove to themselves that they are truly not loved by this person.

This is a common stand. It should be no surprise to us that we demonstrate and express love in our culture the way that we do, with overworking, self-importance, worrying, etc.

Having never questioned our choice or our responsibility in the matter, we are left without hope of changing.

Another common stand is, " I'm Not Good Enough." This can come from a stand in the womb while parents are discussing the sex preference of their child. If you were a boy and your parents wanted a girl, whether spoken or unspoken, most likely your stand would be that you are not good enough. This would show up as bad or inadequate grades in school, being on the second string for football instead of the first, having the same job description as someone else in your office and getting half the pay, being afraid to ask someone on a date that you particularly like, and anything else that you could come up with that would make you feel not good enough.

Everyone who was born that we have worked with so far has a stand. As we said, we tell ourselves over and over again every day of our lives what we think of ourselves, we are not good enough or not wanted or some variation of this stand. It does not necessarily come from just the above circumstances, however. For some, especially the children of today, abortion may have been considered early in the pregnancy — Not Wanted. Money may have been an issue with your parents and they may not have felt that it was the right time to be pregnant — Not loved. Thousands of other circumstances could cause us to take one of these stands.

Most of us, since we have not listened vigilantly to what we tell ourselves hourly about ourselves, do not remember what our stand was at that time. We now feel like the victim of the circumstances and thus think we are powerless to change them.

When we discover that all the events that are happening to us are happening to make us "*right*" about our stand, we can begin to be responsible for the results we are producing. We are no longer powerless to change them. In order to make changes, we must listen to what we are telling ourselves daily.

We gave our word in the beginning with the intensity of our emotions. We made it all up to begin with. We can now look to see how to change our stand to better suit and represent the divine beings that God made us to be.

DISCOVERING OUR STAND

In working with many people, we discovered that the most common stands were:

"I am Not Good Enough"
"I am Not Wanted"
"I am Not Lovable" i.e., not wanted or good enough
"I am The Wrong Sex" i.e., not good enough

To discover your stand, read each of those statements to see which one sounds the most "Right" to you. Be sure to be honest with yourself. Remember that you need to jerk your collar every now and then to get your mind to stop defending your stand (I'm not good enough, because . . .) or to stop invalidating yourself (You're right, I'll never amount to anything, because . . .).

When you find your stand you can see how that statement filters throughout your entire life. If your original stand is "I'm not good enough," you will be not good enough in your job, in your marriage, in your family, in your school, in the financial world, and in all areas of your life. It has been, so far, the foundation of your life; the window through which you see the world. Someone will acknowledge you for a good job and you will think, "Yeah, if only they knew." It is like our lives are built on quicksand. Whenever life gets too good, we pull in some evidence to prove to ourselves that we are right, we aren't good enough, or whatever our stand is.

No matter how good you are, no matter how well you do, you will not allow yourself to be acknowledged. We mean truly acknowledged. Acknowledged with all your heart and soul. This will be true as long as you have the stand that you do.

For us to believe that we are good enough when someone tells us we are would make us a liar about what we said about ourselves. Instead of being a liar, we believe the person acknowledging us just does not know any better.

Is this all starting to sound familiar?

This stand that we have taken is made up by our mind — which, by design, is for our survival. The survival functions of our mind are:

1. To make us right and everyone else wrong.

"Nobody loves me," letting everyone who says they love us know that we do not believe them.

2.   When we are wrong, it justifies our being wrong.

"Of course I did not have a date. Nobody loves me."

3.   To give us all the reasons why it will not work.

"I am not smart enough to go out with him.

4.   To give us all the reasons why it will work.

"I passed the test last year and it was much harder than this one. I can do it!"

We have what we term selective listening. That is, we have a *choice* about which function of the mind we listen to. Do we listen to why we can, why we can't, why we're right or why we're right about being wrong? Most often we listen to why we are right and everyone else is wrong.

Our mind, whose job is our survival (breathing, not walking into doors, heartbeat functions, etc.) made up our original stand, in order to survive. In the midst of the upsetting event, we had to take a stand in order to keep living. In the midst of the upsetting event, we were sure that we were going to die — either emotionally, physically or spiritually. Rather than do that, we took a stand about the way the world was to justify why we should live. We believe, unquestioningly, that we must be right about our stand about ourselves in order to continue to survive. As such, we have been surviving, rather than living.

It is time for us to start living this joyous life that God so graciously gave us to its fullest potential.

In order to do that, we must complete our stand.

COMPLETING OUR STAND

Completing our stand is essential to our Aliveness. "Completion," as used here, means to make whole and complete. Since the time that we took our stand, we have not expressed ourselves as being whole and complete in our lives. There has always been something else that we had to do to be OK, some other degree, some other raise, some other car, some other relationship, etc.

Consider our life as a train and our stand about life as the tracks that the train runs on. Until we change the direction of the tracks that the train runs on, we cannot change the direction of the train. Completing our stand is like changing the direction of the tracks and in some cases like laying a new track. This can be an exciting change. To change the tracks or the direction of the tracks and build a firm foundation for our life, the following methods are suggested to be effective:

1. Make a list of all the times we have been right about our stand, going back as far as we can remember. See if we can recall the original upsetting event out of which we took the stand.

   The time that we did not get chosen as a cheerleader, did not get asked to the prom, did not date much. Look for the things that point to the stand "I am not good enough."

2. After making this list, open your heart to allow yourself to experience what these upsetting events felt like emotionally during the event itself. What was present during that event? Anger, frustration, pain,

fear — how did it feel?

3.   While in the experience of the emotions, declare with
      intensity, that you are now complete with that stand!
      Then take a stand that serves your aliveness so that
      your new track will be laid.

      If your stand was that you were not wanted, you may
      want to take a new stand that you ARE loved and
      wanted.

The important thing in taking a new stand is that it
must be taken in the midst of an emotion. The power of
the word and the intensity of the emotion act like cement
to firmly set the foundation of your stand. This explains
why you can use affirmations or take new stands and have
them work for only a short time. It is important to have
the intensity of the emotion along with the power of your
word.

This also suggests that anytime you are in the midst
of any emotion — love, hate, fear, joy, ecstasy, grief —
any emotion, you can use it to take a new stand about
whatever you are emoting about. So if you are upset
about not having enough money, the time to take a new
stand about how money will work for you is in the midst
of your upset about money. THE POWER TO COM-
PLETE OUR STAND IS GENERATED BY DECLARING
OURSELVES COMPLETE IN THE EXPERIENCE OF
ANY STRONG EMOTION AND TAKING A NEW
STAND IN THE MIDST OF THAT EMOTION!!

Our experience has shown that, for many of us, our
original event or stand was taken at conception, in the
womb or at childbirth. Sometimes we may have difficulty
in recalling that event and the emotions surrounding the
event.

We recommend that if while reading this book you have a strong emotion, you use that emotion to complete your stand. Then take a new one.

TAKING A NEW STAND

After we have completed our stand, we have a firm foundation on which to build a new stand. This new stand is one which can change the direction of the tracks on which the train called our life is headed. We suggest you use the following methods to create the new stand, which we call "The Alivened Stand":

1. Make a list of all the most positive qualities you would like to express in your life. The way you really want to be in the world!

2. Arrange these qualities into a powerful and concise statement that is easy for you to remember.

3. Generate the emotions of love, praise and gratitude very powerfully in your body. While experiencing these, declare with intensity your "Alivened Stand"!!!!

4. Write your "Alivened Stand" on a 3x5 card and repeat it several times a day. Be sure to repeat it with Love, Praise and Gratitude in your heart until you have it fully ingrained into your life and consciousness — Hook, Line and Thinker.

5. Consciously choose to think of yourself always from the point of view of your new stand. Never indulge yourself in thinking about not being good enough or unloved.

6.   Know that YOU ARE A MIRACLE and treat yourself as one.

We wish to illuminate the importance of completing
your stand. We pray that you will see yourself as valuable
enough to take the time to do so.

Following these exercises makes a tremendous shift
in your life as you continue to declare yourself and affirm
your "Alivened Stand."

There is a phenomenon that happens once you take a
stand that you should be aware of. Whenever you take a
stand for something new, your mind will test you to see if
you really mean it and are intending to persist with it.
What this means is, that once you take a new stand, you
must be persistent in integrating that stand. Your mind
will have a tendency to invalidate it and will fight you
against changing. Remember, our old stand, "change
equals danger," is a familiar friend, and our minds resist
change. So, as evidence comes up to make yourself right
about your old stand, keep declaring your new stand as
the right "Alivened Stand."

When we first took our new "Alivened Stand" everything that could come up to prove to us that we were still
"Not Good Enough" did. We kept declaring that, " We
Are Good Enough" with persistence, determination, and
intensity — until our minds finally accepted that we are
good enough to have, do or be anything that we choose.
Keep looking for evidence that you ARE good enough and
eventually the good will prevail.

Just keep reminding yourself that you are a miracle
on this planet and that "God don't make no junk."

OTHER STANDS

During the course of our lives we have taken many stands. We have a stand about money and the way it is. We have a stand about relationships and the way they work or do not work. We have a stand about sex and the way it is. We have a stand about working or not working and what that is. We have a stand about education and whether it is good or bad, etc. All these stands were taken in the midst of an emotional upset. In all areas of our lives, these stands make us right about our original stand; the one taken at conception, in the womb at childbirth, or early childhood. Every new stand that we take moves us closer to being right about our original stand. One couple shared their stands about money with us that serve as an example of how this works. The husband's stand was that all women wanted him for was his money. He was proving that he was not wanted for just being himself. The wife's stand was that no man could take care of her as well as she could take care of herself. She was proving that - she was not loved, because money meant love to her. In order to prove themselves right about not being loved or wanted, the husband, who was a salesman for a solar company that worked strictly on commission, did not sell anything for five months . . . thus bringing in no money. The wife worked to support him and the children until he saw that he was testing to see if all she wanted was his money. When he had no money and she was still around, it made him a liar about his stand. because she is a woman, he had no money and she was still with him. She was proving her stand, that no man could support her the way that she could support herself, by supporting the whole family while he could not.

Both of their stands made their original stand, "I'm not wanted," right. When they discovered this, they declared themselves complete in the midst of their emotions with intensity and have since taken new stands with intensity. Money is in abundance on this planet.

They now have an overabundance of love, money, sex and joy in their lives. So be it.

Once you complete your original stand, you will start to become conscious of your other stands. You will have knocked the foundation out from under the other stands. Then a domino effect will start to occur. It may be exciting to you when this starts to happen. Your mind will use anything to keep you in your stand. Every time you feel fearful about the changes, think of the excitement of having your life be the way you have always wanted it to be.

Think of the joy, harmony, effortlessness, and ecstasy that your "Alivened Stand" will bring, not only to you, but to others — as you keep declaring your life as a miracle.

The only pitfall, if there is one in this whole matter of stands, is that some people will want to blame their parents, grandparents, doctors, anesthesiologists and whomever for their stand. Remember, it was *you* who said the way it would be for you. No matter what happened to you, you are the one who said the way it was. It was not necessarily the way you thought it was, however.

We know people who believe that their childhood was the most disastrous of all. Once they became responsible for the stand they took, they saw that they never *allowed* their parents to love them, even though their parents did truly love them.

In families with multiple siblings, each of them has their own story of how it was, growing up in their family. In talking with them, you would think they were from several different families, because they all have their own stands through which they see the world.

We all see life through our own stands — what we said about how the world would be. Until we complete our stands, we will continue to believe that we are less than we are.

Our perception of life is our responsibility. We can live life daily as a burden, or we can live life daily as a miracle. God has given us all the powers to make paradise on this planet. *We* are the ones who get to choose now how it will be. Let us choose Aliveness!

There is not a moment in which
his voice fails to direct my
thoughts, guide my actions, and
lead my feet. I am walking
steadily on toward truth. W,99

CHAPTER 4

CYCLES AND PATTERNS

Some people do not take a stand about their life until another child is born into the family, often when they are one to two years old.

Another way to determine what your stand is, is to discover *when* you took your stand — hence this chapter.

We live our lives in a pattern and a cycle. The same kinds of events or similar kinds of events happen to us over and over again until we can no longer call them coincidences.

These patterns happen in a time frame. In other words, they have a particular cycle in time as well as similar circumstances. These patterns were started when we took our original stand and have been acted out in the same time frame over and over — year after year.

Whatever age we were when we took our stand determines what the recurring time cycle will be in our life. For example, if you were two months in utero when you found out that your mother wanted a boy instead of a girl; you would have taken a stand that you were not good enough. Your cycle would be two. Your pattern would be proving that you are not good enough because you thought you were the wrong sex.

This cycle can be two hours, two days, two years or any multiple of two. It could be four, six, eight, ten, etc. The most powerful event would happen on the multiple of itself. For example if your pattern is two, the strongest would be two times two, or four, and four times four, or sixteen, and so on.

What this means is that we recreate a tremendous upset on the birthday, if you will, of our original stand and we do it unconsciously, without choice. A good example is a girl we once worked with who discovered her pattern was to get pregnant and have an abortion every two years. She had no idea that it was a pattern. Recalling the abortions was painful for her. Therefore, she had never noticed the time span between the abortions. She had an abortion every two years for five cycles (ten years). So every other year for ten years she got pregnant and had an abortion. In the Weekend, she discovered that her mother had tried, unsuccessfully, to abort her when she was two months in the womb. She recalled the terror, grief, and anger at her mother that she had experienced during this event. She was acting out this pattern of abortion over and over, unconsciously, in her pattern (two years) just like clockwork. After discovering and completing her pattern, she soon got married, pregnant (right in her pattern) and is now a happy mother of a beautiful baby boy. This time she did not act out the pattern.

Another person we worked with, also had a pattern of two years. This man ended his relationships every two years. He was also fired every four years from every job he had ever had — four being the strongest due to the 2x2 factor.

Others we have known stay in relationships for their patterns (two years) and then leave their relationships to fulfill their patterns (at the end of two years).

A friend of ours had a five year pattern which was very clear to him. He was married for 25 years and ended his relationship with his wife around their anniversary, acting out his pattern. Again the 5x5 factor was the strongest.

Are we saying this is necessary? No. We are saying that most of us are unconscious of it. While we may be choosing to do things such as ending our relationships, perhaps it is nothing more than acting our original stand out through our pattern. Anything that takes away our choices in this life and leaves us feeling powerless is worth getting rid of. Our unconscious patterns leave us powerless. It is time to regain our power through consciousness of our patterns.

FINDING YOUR PATTERNS

It is important for you to discover what your patterns are in order to be responsible for them. Most people feel the victim of their patterns, or controlled by them. You only have control of something when you have consciousness about it. The following exercise has assisted many in uncovering for themselves what their pattern is:

1.   Make a chronological list, by year and month of all
     the major, life changing or very upsetting events that
     have occurred throughout your lifetime. You can
     either start at birth and go forward or you can start
     at the present and go backward in time.

Major upsetting or life changing events can be
pleasant events such as: having children, getting married,
going on a world cruise, graduating college or high school,
sending your child off to kindergarten, getting the home
of your dreams, etc. Anything that changes the status quo
is considered an upsetting event. Other events that cause
us to take stands are: the birth of a sibling after us, the
death of a loved one, separation or divorce in our family,
moving to a new home and separation from our friends,
illness, accidents, change of jobs, loss of jobs, having a
child leave home and any number of upsetting losses.

2.   Once you have made your list, open yourself up to
     discover what your pattern is and how often the
     cycle repeats itself. This may take some searching.
     Everyone we have worked with has a pattern. Just
     know that your mind is invested in NOT discovering
     this because it took the stand to survive. Be vigilant
     with yourself until you can determine what the com-
     mon denominator is in your pattern. When you dis-
     cover how often your cycle repeats itself you will
     know how old you were when you took your stand.
     This makes it easier to uncover the circumstances
     that were so upsetting at that age. For example if
     your pattern is two, find out what happened at two
     that was upsetting enough to take a stand about. If
     you cannot find it there, then try two months after
     birth or two months in the womb. You will find it if
     you keep being vigilant with your mind.

For some people, their pattern is in months. To them, it looks like they are upset *all* the time. If you keep looking you will find a particular month or yearly pattern.

Many people have certain months of the year in which they have their upsets. The most commonly upsetting months are our birth month, our conception month, or the month in which a sibling is born after us. Look at your patterns to see if you have a particularly eventful month of the year when your upsets happen.

So now what? Now that we know we have a pattern, what can we do about it? Like your stand, you can complete it.

COMPLETING PATTERNS

Remember that *completing* something means to make it whole. Your pattern has served as a reminder to you that the stand you took at the age of your pattern is truly the right stand for you. You must complete it to complete your stand. We operate our lives in this cycle and pattern due to our stand. We no longer need to continually act it out since we have rid ourselves of our stand. To complete cycles and patterns, we offer the following suggestions:

1. Clearly define your pattern and the cycle it operates in. Then identify yourself and your stand as the source in the matter. This means that *you* took the stand which set into motion the cycles and patterns. You may start to see how powerful your word is at this point.

2. Take 100% responsibility (accountability) for all the events that have happened to make you right about what your stand is. Since the cycle only serves to remind you that the original stand you took was

right, you can see that the circumstances were brought forth to make you right, again.

3.   Open your heart to experience the grief that you have caused to those who loved you and were hurt by you acting out your stand. The girl who had the abortion not only was guilty and devastated by the abortions, but by the number of men whom were hurt as a result of her actions. When experiencing the pain, and taking a new stand in the midst of that pain, she completed her stand. So, in the midst of the experience of those who have been hurt by your actions due to your cycles and patterns, declare yourself complete with your stands. Declare a new stand that will bring you more positive results in your life and in the lives of those around you.

The pitfall, as we have called it, in having this information, is that some people use it to validate how bad they have been or how wrong they have been in the past. This will keep you in your pattern. All there is to do is — to experience the grief you have caused others through your unconsciousness. Then do whatever you can to correct it. Remember, anytime you fall victim to anything, you give your power to that thing, person or circumstance. Keep reminding yourself that you are a miracle of life.

PLANNING YOUR PATTERNS

At this point you should be clear about your pattern and cycle and which months most of your upsets occur. We now suggest that rather than resisting your patterns, you plan them.

The times of your pattern are very powerful. You may as well plan for it to be exciting, rather than have the universe pick an upset to make your original stand right.

Something will happen in that time allotted if you do not plan it, so you may as well choose to plan it for yourself.

For the two of us, our most upsetting time was in February every year. Yes, we had a yearly pattern. Every year in February we have had upsetting events happen. February is the month of our conceptions. We have been acting out our stands taken at conception. Since we are now conscious of our patterns, we now take great care in planning our upsetting events. One year we bought a car when it seemed like we could not afford it. Another year we bought a piece of jewelry that it also seemed we could not afford. Another year we bought a new home under the same circumstances. The year after that we got married, had 210 guests at our reception and went to Maui for our honeymoon, all under the same conditions. It has been so much fun to plan our patterns (and they always happen when we plan them in February) that we are starting to really enjoy February, finally. Before we started planning them, one of us would get get ill or physically injured. It was frightening when we started looking at the patterns and trying to discover a way out of the automaticity of it.

So, all of the events that we planned; our wedding, car, home, etc.; were upsetting in that they cost us a lot of money that it looked like we had no way to earn. Our upset was acted out. We needed to find ways to make the things happen, and we had a positive result come out of our upsets. This is the purpose for planning our cycles and patterns.

To plan your patterns and cycles, we offer the following exercise which we use at least once a year:

1. From your list of cycles and patterns, determine which months are your most upsetting months. Be clear that this is your pattern and your cycle, and

you can be responsible for choosing your upset.

2.   Now, actively plan how you will fulfill your pattern
        in a positive way. Take a trip to the islands, go on a
        cruise, buy a new car. Stay aware of your pattern
        and know that when you start to get upset that what
        you are upset about is your pattern of the past. It
        has nothing to do with what is going on now.

We know of a person whose pattern is to leave his
wife every two years. He seemingly had no control over
it. When he hit his pattern of two, he was out the door
with his suitcase and off to pick up someone else. He
decided he was not going to do this anymore. He started
looking for ways to fulfill the pattern in a more positive
manner, since he was in touch with how painful it was to
his relationship when he left. He decided to leave her
during the pattern and meet her at a bar and pick her up
just as he had been doing with other women every two
years for several years. This acted out the pattern and no
one was damaged by it. They vacationed together for a
week and then he would leave her and go home separately.
It was a brilliant idea. They got to vacation together,
which they both enjoyed, and to rediscover each other
during their week long "fling."

We know of another couple who discovered they had
upsets daily at 8:45 a.m., 5:15 p.m. and 10:45 p.m. Every
day during their married lives, they would fight and argue
over little things, at those times of the day. When they
started looking for the pattern in their arguments, they
discovered the times. They related it to their family.
They found that the upsets came from when their dads
went to work, came home from work and right before
bedtime.

They made an agreement with each other to not fight during those times. It was difficult at first because it was an unconscious pattern. Through their vigilance and persistence, one or the other of them would look at the time when they started arguing. They discovered that it was just their pattern.

It has now turned into a joke. Whenever they begin to argue, you see them both going for their watches.

FAMILY PATTERNS

What most people do not realize about their parents is — that their parents had parents. This means their parents took a stand and have patterns and cycles just as they do. And their parents had parents who took a stand and had patterns and cycles. All of these patterns and cycles have been handed down, so to speak.

If our parents pattern was two and they acted it out by having children, or moving, or changing jobs, or whatever, every two years, we would take on their pattern. Just as they took on their own parents pattern. This means that our entire family would be in upset at approximately the same time, every time the pattern revealed itself.

Did you ever notice that there are times when your family just seems to be out of whack while the rest of the time they are wonderful? It is because all are in the same pattern, producing upsetting events in order to fulfill the pattern. So, plan your family pattern as well as your individual pattern. Sometimes your pattern will be the same as your family's and sometimes it will not. You will have to research the pattern to find out what it is. Then you can plan for it, just as you did previously.

Remember, your parents and the rest of your family are also miracles.

The one wholly true thought
about the past is that it
is not here.   W,13

CHAPTER 5

JUDGEMENTS AND EVALUATIONS

So far, we have discovered that we gave our word about our life. The result of our word has shown up to give us agreement or validation for what we said. Sometimes, we will even have others tell us what we said — to further prove to ourselves that what we think and say about ourselves is accurate.

Have you listened lately to the things you think about others? Do you know that as soon as you see someone or meet someone that your mind instantly has something to say about that person? The dialogue goes something like, "Isn't she beautiful?", "How ridiculous to wear those socks with those sandals!", "Why is that young girl with that old man? He must have money!", and on and on for *each* person that we notice or meet. We call these thoughts — judgements and evaluations — because what we are doing, when we allow ourselves to have those thoughts, is judging and evaluating someone. It takes only seconds for us to figure out how someone *really* is, according to our judgements and evaluations.

The problem with allowing these thoughts to occur without stopping them, is that once we say how they are, that is it on how they are to us. Since we now know how they are, we expect them to act consistent with the way we think they are. We are not surprised when they act in accord with our thoughts. Remember, your thoughts are powerful, productive, and the basis for your reality. What this means, is that once we judge people and start looking for evidence that our assessment is accurate, they act *for us* the way that we have stated they will.

What is the purpose of this? It keeps us separate from others. Our fear is that if others really knew how we were, in other words, if others knew that we *really* are not good enough, they would not want to be with us. We keep ourselves separate to protect our stand about ourselves, hoping that no one will find out.

You see, while we are proving to ourselves that we are not good enough or are not loved, we are at the same time trying to convince ourselves, and everyone around us, that we really are. Thus; the further education — to PROVE that we are OK, or the bigger boat to PROVE that someone loves us, or the finest clothes to PROVE that . . . . This is the internal struggle that so many of us find ourselves in when we have truly accomplished something that has been very important for us in our lives. The joy and excitement lasts only a day or so. Any longer than that and we pull in some evidence to prove that we still are not good enough.

What do we judge people by? We judge by our own standards, thoughts, and evaluations about *ourselves*. And where do these come from? They come from our stand. Most of our judgements of others are based on whether we think they are better than us or less than us, smarter than us or more ignorant than us, or things like this. We use what we really think about ourselves as the basis for judging others.

One person we know had a stand that she was not wanted. The result of this stand was that she thought she was not beautiful. She was. Everyone told her, but she could not hear it, because she knew that she was not beautiful. The way she judged other women was whether they were prettier than she or not. So, every time she saw a woman, her dialogue was "She's beautiful" or "I am prettier than she." In addition to this, were her judgements about what beautiful meant. She believed that beautiful women were snobs. Since they were more beautiful than she was, they could not possibly want to be with her. . . thus, they must be snobs. OK. So, beautiful women are now snobs.

Do you realize how many truly beautiful women there are in this country alone? Millions! What this meant to her was that she could not or would not befriend anyone who was beautiful by her standards because she *said* that they were snobs. And she was not in the least bit surprised that beautiful women showed up around her as snobs. After all, that is how she expected them to be, and she got what she asked for. She noticed this and thus began affirming that, beautiful women are beautiful to be with. She then began changing her judgements about herself. After doing this, she felt more and more beautiful and allowed herself to be surrounded by beautiful women.

Out of changing her original stand, it was easy for her to start changing her judgements about her physical appearance.

To discover what your judgements are, not only about yourself, but especially about others, we offer the following:

1.   Write the statement: "What keeps me from being in love with you is _____." Fill in the blank for each person that you know. Notice what your recurring judgements are and how they relate to you. Do you judge others according to appearance, personality, etc.? This gives you a clue as to where you judge yourself harshly. If you are judging others, you can bet that you are judging yourself in the same manner.

2.   Notice how right you are about what you said about those people. The judgements we *make up* in our mind are as real to us as the sun rising every day.

Since most of us judge others based on what we believe to be the truth about us, and whether they are better than us or less than us, we are continuously comparing ourselves with them.

3.   Now write or ask yourself, "If this is not the truth about them; what is?" You may discover that you really do not know who people are. All we know about people is what we said about them, which we are being right about. We made it all up to make ourselves right about being separate and protected and safe.

Do you ever have the experience of thinking someone is just terrible when you first meet them, and then after a short time they become your best friend? Or someone that you think would never be interested in you, calls you and asks you out to lunch? You can see that your judgements are made solely to keep you separate from others.

When you begin to change the way you *think* about yourself, and examine with what standards you judge others; you can then become responsible for your judgements and choose what it is you want to say about yourself as well as others.

You will be right about whatever you say, so why not choose to say something that enlivens others when you are around them?

JUDGEMENTS ABOUT OUR BODIES

Not only do we have judgements about our personality, humor, and intelligence; we also have judgements about our body.

In this age of body consciousness, with all the new diets, physical fitness regimes, and consciousness pertaining to lengthening our stay here on this planet (physical immortality), most of us have become very concerned about the way our bodies are.

Again, we use others' bodies to compare with our bodies. We are, either, better than or not as good as most of the bodies that we see.

As always, we are accurate in what we say about our bodies. Like all else, our bodies are willing to make us right about what we say about them. How many times a day do we invalidate our human temple? How many times a day do we tell it — it is too fat, too ugly, too thin, too light, too dark, too sickly, too much hair, not enough hair, the wrong color hair, too short, too tall?

What do you think that your body does with that information?

It makes you right, of course. Remember the angel sitting on your shoulder, giving you everything that you ask for? Well, if every time you look in the mirror you tell yourself that you are unattractive, that is what will happen. And if every time you look at your stomach in the mirror you tell yourself that you are fat or getting fat, guess what you will be right about? You got it now.

So, maybe one way to avoid this is to stop looking in the mirror. How is that going to change your thoughts about yourself? Avoidance never changed anything. It just prolongs the situation.

The first thing to do with the judgements you have in the above exercises, is to notice that *you* said your body was imperfect in some way. Perhaps you have collected agreement along the way, with people telling you the same thing that you have been telling yourself, but *it was you* who first said it to yourself.

Next, is for you to discover what you really want to think about your body and start affirming to yourself that your body is that way. Some people say, "Well, that's lying. I am not young, healthy and beautiful. I am fat, sickly and ugly." If you made it up in the first place, you lied to yourself, right? And then you convinced yourself that what you said was true. You can do the same with the "warm fuzzies" and positive thoughts, as you are currently doing with the "cold pricklies," or negative thoughts.

We recommend that you get a full length mirror and examine yourself every day or as often as possible. Keep telling yourself your positive affirmation about your body. Every time you think, "I am fatter than she is," or "He has more hair than I do," just keep repeating over and over again the way your body is becoming. If you can bring yourself to confront the terrible things that you have said about your body, and change these thoughts, you will be amazed at how quickly your body will respond to your demands for health, vigor, vitality and youth.

Another thing that is harmful to your body, are the statements you make about your body in relation to others. Things like "She's a pain in the neck" are said frequently, and people wonder why they have neck pains.

There are books in the recommended reading section, in the back of this book, which cover this topic in more detail. It is well worth discovering what you are saying about your body, for the purpose of continued health and vitality.

Some people who have a stand that they are the wrong sex have tremendous judgements about their body, as you might well imagine. These people like nothing about their body and it shows when you look at them. They very often have major health problems and wind up with hysterectomies (removing the organs that are considered female) or have something else go "wrong" with their body in the areas that mark them as male or female.

The point is that you have judgements, which you continually tell yourself, over and over again, which create or generate an unhealthy, unalivening outcome. It is time to choose to be responsible for your thoughts, judgements and evaluations; and to change them to those thoughts which bring you aliveness, joy and satisfaction.

Remember, your body is your temple — your vehicle for getting around in this life. You would not be here without it. It is as precious to your existence as is your spiritual connection to God. Be kind to it and love it and it will be kind to you and love you.

Have it be OK the way that it is, no matter how it is, and if you want to change things about it, that is fine. Just have it be OK for now just the way that it is, just by *saying* so.

JUDGING OUR BEHAVIOR

In addition to judging our bodies, we also have judged our personalities and behavior. Have you ever done or said something that you really did not mean to say, and someone got hurt? Have you ever said things to your parents, children or spouse that you knew would hurt them, and you said it anyway? It was almost as if you could not help yourself. Most of us have intentionally hurt someone. That is a lot to own. We know. You have already judged yourself for that misdoing.

Most of us have done things that we are not proud of. We have judged ourselves guilty for having treated others the way that we did. We punish ourselves and reinforce the thoughts of how "bad" we really are. As a result, most of our thinking about our personalities and behavior are negative, making us negative.

The key to making yourself whole again is the same as throughout this book: complete it, be responsible for it, communicate it, and then forgive it.

The following may assist you:

1.   Write or think of the statement: "The way that I hurt _____ is that I _____." Use your loved one's name and fill in what you judged yourself as doing that was hurtful.

2.   Now review these statements and find the common thoughts that you have about yourself for having

treated people the way you did.

For example, if you said something unkind and judged yourself as an unkind person you would have no choice but to show up as unkind.

3. It should be clear to us by now, that we are 100% responsible for what we did to ourselves and our loved ones, through our stand about ourselves and our lives. All that is left, when we are fully responsible for any situation, is to communicate with our loved ones, apologize for what we have done, and promise we will not treat them unkindly or disrespectfully again.

4. Having completed the communication with them and apologized to them, the only thing left for us to do is to *forgive ourselves* for allowing ourselves to treat our loved ones the way we deemed inappropriate. Then promise ourselves that we will manage our judgements about our behavior in a more positive way, so we can begin to produce a more positive behavior.

Completing this exercise will free us from all the guilt, shame, and blame that we have about ourselves for what we have done to others in the past. This will allow us to start to love ourselves *just the way we are.*

It is time for us to start praising ourselves and loving ourselves, so we can be free to love, honor and respect others.

All any of us want is to love and be loved. Start to affirm to yourself that you are loving and loved and that you are a perfect creation of a loving Father.

JUDGEMENTS ABOUT PARENTS AND PARTNERS

Since we have been judging and evaluating everyone and everything, our parents and partners are no exception. We have been doing the same to them.

When we were young, we made up judgements about how our parents were and we have been right about those judgements, as we saw in the previous exercises. Some may say, "Yeah, but my parents are that way." If we took 100 people off the street who knew your parents, do you believe that they would feel the same way about your parents that you do? Usually one parent is good and the other is bad, for whatever justification we have invented. It makes no difference what the justification is, it just makes a difference that we *said* so, and that is the way it is for us.

In the next chapter you will have an opportunity to examine and complete what you said about your parents. The important thing to examine right now is the judgements you made about your parents' relationship with each other. What judgements did you make about the way that your parents expressed their love for each other?

Whatever judgement you made about the way that your parents expressed their love to each other and to you, you will be right about. If your parents yelled and screamed at each other, loving you would involve a lot of screaming and yelling, because, to you loving equals yelling and screaming. If your spouse judged that the way to be loved was to be quiet and gentle, because that was how they (parents) expressed their love for one another, your spouse would require quiet and gentleness in order to feel loved, because quiet and gentle equals love to them.

Can you see the conflict that could arise in this situation? One of you needs to be quiet and gentle in order to feel loved and one of you needs to be yelled at and screamed at in order to feel loved. Quite a dilemma.

The thing to do is to discover what you judge to be love. How do you know that you are loved? Now that you have completed your stand and know that you *can* love and *are* loved, how will you express it?

When you are aware of your family patterns and the judgements you made about "family" through interacting with your family, you can be responsible for the judgements — rather than living your life as if they were true. Who wants to be in love with someone who believes that love requires a lot of yelling and screaming? Not that it is bad to yell and scream, just that it is unnecessary to do so in order to feel loved. You are loved. You do not need to do anything but discover your judgements about how someone should love you in order for them to fulfill your need and for you to complete your judgement.

As we can see, most of our life is lived from a reaction to something in the past. Knowing that the upset is from the past and not about the present, helps you to let go and not take your anger out on the ones you love.

Just examine your family life and compare it to the way your life is now. More often than not, you will be living just like your family — or exactly opposite of your family. They were either right about their lives — or they were wrong about their lives — in *your* opinion.

Whatever we are incomplete about in our relationships with our family, we will reenact in our relationship with our spouses. This is why it is so important for us to discover what we have said about our parents, and complete it.

JUDGEMENTS ABOUT GOD

One of the things that most of us have never questioned is our relationship with and judgements about God. As we were growing up, we judged our parents' relationship with God and made their relationship right or wrong. For most of us, God has to do with some force outside of ourselves that is something to be feared. Very often we hear, "God will get you," or "Avoid God's wrath," as a child.

For the most part, our judgements have to do with some type of religious background. We either liked our church or did not. We made judgements about God based on our judgements about our church. If someone died in our family and we blamed God for taking them, on some level we would perceive God as unfair or cruel.

Since most people learned about God as being outside themselves, they have never examined their hearts in order to truly open up to discover who God is for them. And to discover how much He/She loves them.

When you have no spiritual connection to God, or a spiritual force that most call God, you feel that no matter what you have, you are still a bit empty. What is missing is your spiritual connection.

We are not talking here about religion. The purpose of all religion is to bring us to a spiritual awakening, no matter what the denomination.

What we are talking about is God. This is the spiritual force that resides in your heart or soul, or wherever you believe it to be. We are talking about that connection to your divinity that for many of us has been void for many years.

God is not out to get anyone. He/She is ever present to remind us of the divine beings that we are and can become. All we have to do is to examine and complete the stand we have about who we *think* God is, and open our hearts to discover for ourselves who God really is.

If we have a particular Church or Synagogue that we attend which brings us closer to God, we feel that ours is the only way to get closer to God. We take this stand to make ourselves right about what we are saying about God, and thus make any other way of thinking about or experiencing God, wrong. We say "I am Catholic" or "I am Jewish" or "I am Christian," and our religion then becomes the one to follow. Do we really believe that there is just one way to reach God? Well, we do not think so.

We know that our religion is a stand that we took about what was right FOR US. What is right for us, is not necessarily the only right way for every human being on this planet. So, complete your stand about there only being one way to discover who God is, and allow people to use whatever way they feel guided to discover God.

As long as people discover God, what difference does it make to any of us, how or where they found Him/Her?

We personally support everyone in being everything that they want. If this is Catholic, fine; Protestant, fine; Jewish, fine; Christian, fine. It does not matter. As long as we live what God teaches *from our heart*, we cannot possibly find fault with others' point of view. Can we? There are no wrong religions.

We use our judgements about others' religions to keep us separate, as you may have discovered in the earlier process. If you can bring yourself to question this highly sensitive issue and complete the judgements about God, and what is true about Him/Her for you, you can choose to be with whomever you please, whatever religion you please, without having to judge people by their beliefs. Believe whatever you want about God after you have opened your heart. Do not, however, expect others to have the same experience as you do. Their connection is not any better or worse than yours, just because they are a different religion or belief system.

It is time for us to stop the religious wars on our planet and begin *living* God's work, rather than just talking about it. Love your neighbor *and* yourself, and see what happens.

Know that God resides in your heart for all time, through all circumstances. All you have to do is, open your heart to receive Him/Her.

DO YOUR JUDGEMENTS SERVE YOU

This is a good question, huh? "Do your judgements serve you?" At first your answer may be "No, no way!" Well, up until now, they did. They served to keep you separate. They served to make your stand right. They served to keep you unconscious of the beauty of God and His/Her children.

Perhaps the question should be, "Do these judgements bring us more Alive?" It is a good question to ponder. If what you give you get back multiplied; is what you have been putting out, what you want to get back multiplied? We think not.

We believe that all people want is to love and be loved. The problem is most people have so many judgements about themselves that they feel unworthy. Even the toughest people can turn into warm, compassionate beings, after letting love come in to their lives.

Begin to monitor your negative "cold pricklies" and whenever you catch one, just cancel the thought, and replace it with a "warm fuzzy," a warm, naturally loving thought.

As we said before, we will always be right about what we say about situations. Think the highest possible thoughts and produce the highest possible results in our lives!

Should you choose to focus all of your thoughts on Love, Praise and Gratitude for all things, miracles will become a natural occurrence as "What you sow, so shall ye reap."

> *Only one equal gift can be*
> *offered to the equal sons*
> *of God, and that is full*
> *appreciation!   T,97*

CHAPTER 6

PARENTS

As we stated earlier, we have things that we made up, early in life, about our parents and our own particular truths about them. As we can see by this time, most of what we made up are untruths which have made us right about our stand.

We can only see our parents through the stand which serves as a filter. This being the case, most of us do not know who our parents are.

If we have explored awareness and consciousness activities, we may believe that we are fine with our parents. Usually what we do, however, is complete with our parents and transfer our upset from our parents to our spouse. Our relationship with our parents is now fine, but our spouse is seeming every day more and more the way we used to think about our parents.

Our negative judgements become clearer when we become parents and begin to understand the difficulty and concern that goes with parenting.

The only way out is to examine the judgements we used to have about our parents, freshly, as if we had never done it before, and to discover to whom we have transferred our judgements.

For this purpose, we offer the following suggestion:

1. Write the following statement: "The truth about my mother was _____." (She was loving, she was dominant, etc.) This list should be how you thought about her when you were growing up.

2. Now review the list and notice what your stand was about your mom. What were you being right about? Notice how she always seemed to be that way to you.

3. Begin again now with a new statement: "If what I say is true about my mom is really a lie, what is the truth about my mom?"

The answer will always be that she loved you with all her heart and soul. She gave you everything that she could to be sure that you turned out successful, loving and caring. That is not to say that she did it the way *you* said she should do it. If your stand was that you were not wanted, no matter how much she tried to let you know she loved you, you would not have been able to let the love in, because you would have to be a liar. So you would keep her at a distance and say that she did not love you, to make your stand right.

Now open your heart to discover how your mom really feels about you and how you really feel about her.

Parents and children love each other, no matter what has happened in the past. You love each other no matter what you think. If you will open your heart to that, you can discover just how strong your love is!

Now repeat the same exercise for your dad.

Open your heart to listen to what your heart has to say about how you feel about your dad. You may think he was not there for you. He may not have been there physically, but he was working to give you all that he felt you needed. If you look for the times when he was there for you, and open your heart to discover how you truly feel about your dad, you will discover just how much he loves you and you love him. Regardless of what judgements and evaluations you have about each other, open your heart and let the love wash away the judgements.

We are talking about your heart here. Remember that the only way to complete something is through the power of your word AND the intensity of your emotions. Whatever emotions you choose to use are fine — but an emotion *must* be present.

We know someone who had not seen her father for eight years who did this process. She fell deeply in love with her father and discovered that he was not the monster that she had thought he was. What she realized, was that she was so judgmental of him that there was no way he could love her. She would not let him get close to her for fear that he would find out that she was not loveable.

We know someone else who could not stand being around her mother, whom she felt was the dominant figure in the household. When she opened her heart, she discovered that her mother was concerned for her well-being and was overprotective due to the fear of losing her. She saw how much her mom really loved her.

Listen, your parents may have made some mistakes. SO WHAT? Who cares? Who on this earth is so perfect that they always know how to read our minds and give us what we want? Where do you think they got their knowledge about being parents? From their parents. And where did they get it from? Their parents. All you can do is acknowledge your parents for never giving up on you, and for always loving you, no matter what you did to shut them out. Forgive yourself for not allowing yourself to be loved for all these years.

And if you are a parent, forgive yourself for those things that you have judged wrong in raising your kids. Kids turn out by their stand, as we shall see. Acknowledge yourself for having done as good a job as you did.

PARENTAL APPROVAL

All through our lives, whether we like our parents or not, we have been doing everything we can to win their approval (to be good enough in their eyes). We never thought we were approved of, due to our stand. Now that our stand is complete, we are left with the sadness of how many times we felt our parents did not approve of us. We do not really even know if they did or not. Most of us never asked them.

The truth is that most of us do not approve of ourselves. We cannot, therefore, see how much our parents *do* approve of us and are proud of us. Even if they never spoke it to us, we know they approve. We walk around, feeling unloved and unapproved of by most everyone —

especially the ones we love the most. If they say they approve of us we get awkward and embarrassed and say, "It was nothing." This is because it makes our stand, that we are not good enough, wrong and it is embarrassing to be wrong.

You may begin to see that with all of our judgements about our parents, we really do not know who they are. Our judgements have nothing at all to do with how our parents really are. Our judgements are merely the blinders we have on in order to keep us separate from them. Do you know your parents' hopes, do you know their dreams, do you know what they would want if they could have anything in this world? Do you give them all that you can to be sure they have what they want? Or have you only been interested in what you want or need *from* them?

The difference between children and adults is that children take, take, take and take some more until there is nothing left to take — and then they take some more. Anyone who has a two-year old can plainly see this. Adults give, give, give and give some more, until there is nothing left to give — and then they give some more. Most of us have been taking all of our lives and have forgotten how to give back to our parents. It is time to discover who your parents are and to begin giving back to them the aliveness and life they gave to you.

Most often, all parents want to know is that their children have turned out all right, that they have done a good job, and that their children are thankful to have them as parents. Parents just want to know that they are OK. Most of us will not give this to our parents, because we are afraid that we would lose them. We fear we would no longer be able to lean on them for support, or to call and have them fix our troubles.

Our parents do love us and we do love our parents. The only thing that has kept us from expressing and experiencing that love, is what we made up about them. Would it be worth giving up your judgements if you knew that you could, right this minute, fall back in love with your parents? Of course it would.

We offer the following suggestions:

1. Develop a clear concise statement completing the past with your parents and stating how it is and will continue to be, no matter what judgements you may have. Such as, "My parents love me more and more each day. Our love is growing in every way."

2. Now generate the feelings of Love, Praise and Gratitude for your parents. In the midst of the intensity of these feelings, declare your statement about your relationship with them. Know that this is your new truth.

3. Call them and tell them you love them. Send them flowers or a card declaring your appreciation of all they put up with from you. If they have passed on, just speak it out loud and know that they have heard you.

PARENTS AS MODELS

Since we had judgements and evaluations about our parents and the way they lived life, we have to some extent used them as models to mold our lives. If we disapproved of the way they did life, we will do life just the opposite. If we approved of the way they did life, we will do life just like they did it. As much as we disliked the way things were done, we will still model ourselves after them, as well as treat our family in the same manner. This has been discovered over and over again with families of alcoholics, abusive spouses, and abusive parents.

We may not act this out the way our parents did. Perhaps we do not physically abuse our children, but more than likely emotionally or verbally, we do. Just as our parents felt bad and guilty about doing this, so do we. When we list the characteristics and dynamics of our family, it becomes very clear to us that we did in fact model our family after our parents' family.

1. List all of the qualities and actions of your parents that you disliked or think were wrong. Notice the judgements that you have about these actions.

2   Now make a list of all the qualities and actions that you have and dislike about yourself that you think are wrong. Notice the judgements you have about yourself for these actions.

3   Now forgive your parents and yourself for the judgements you have had and declare yourself complete with your stands about how families are. Take a new stand that will have your family be alive, joyful, and in love.

In reviewing these lists, are you acting like your parents acted or just opposite? Do you have a choice in the matter?

A dynamic that happens very often in families is choosing sides. We pick one parent, and they are the one for us. We make them right all the way, or we fight with them all the way. At any rate, they are the one for us. The other is tolerated. Remember how it was growing up. Which parent did you like the best?

The bond that happens during parenting, especially when one spouse spends their time defending a child, is similar to a marriage. When you consider this, notice which parent you are married to. If your mom or dad are married to you, how can they be married to each other? Set your parents free. Divorce them both. Let them fall in love with each other again and discover who they are, without you in the middle.

Parents are people too. As such, they have a right to be loved, nurtured and acknowledged. Have you hugged your parents today?

Everything you teach you
are learning. Teach only
Love, and learn that Love
is yours and you are Love!
T,92

CHAPTER 7

CHILDREN

We believe that children are sent to heal us. Children are here to teach us to laugh, to play, to love, to trust each other, to teach us to hug more, and to do lots of wonderful loving things that our planet desperately needs right now. For the most part, kids are wonderful little people to be around. We know that communicating with infants and newborns and babies in the womb are all new possibilities. We are excited at the new birthing methods, underwater deliveries, and other gentler methods of being brought into our beautiful world.

As it is, however, our children also have a stand about the world, and are not always the easiest people to love. Their little minds are doing the same thing that we have been talking about throughout this entire book.

The way that children act out their "I'm not good enough — Oh, yes I am!" is through attaching themselves to one parent. Usually little boys attach to their moms and little girls to their dads. Before the parents know it, they are arguing over the fairness of how to discipline, raise, teach, feed, or something else about the child. Huge arguments have been had over the littlest things that make no difference. And the parents cannot figure out why their relationship went sour "after the baby came."

Children are powerful little beings, just like we are. They have given their word about the way their world is and they are determined to make themselves right about it. Just as we were. They know exactly how to get spouses to start fighting. The story goes something like this: "When I was young I would ask my mom if I could do something, knowing she would say 'ask your father,' then I would ask my father, knowing he would say 'ask your mother.' I would keep doing this, not letting the other one know that I was doing it, until finally they exploded at each other about whose responsibility I was. When Mom would go to her room angry, I would have Dad *all to myself*. Mission accomplished."

Now, multiply that kind of shenanigan times the number of children in the family, and we've got big, big trouble.

It is important that we remain open to hear this information. With the divorce rate doubling in this country, we must start looking for some answers to our problems.

As parents, we have noticed how well behaved our children are when alone with one or the other of us; but when our spouse comes home, they start acting up until we get upset and wind up fighting with each other.

Children, because of their stands, feel that the only way to get love is to divide and conquer — to get one parent and the other siblings out of the way (sibling rivalry), so they can be alone with whichever parent they are after. Parents put up with it because "They are only children."

Children have a lot of power in our relationships *if* we let them. When we are incomplete with how we tried to split up our parents we cannot possibly see how our children are trying to split us up.

This is not always a conscious act on the child's part, by the way. If the parents completed their relationships with their parents, and were responsible for the subtle ways in which they tried to get their parents apart, they would be able to see these things in their own children and communicate about them before jeopardizing their own relationship.

Parents' major fear is that they will not be a good parent. This is from their judging their parents as bad parents, or from looking for approval. Some of us are so committed to looking good as a parent, that we actually betray (lie to) our spouse. Then our child will like us and we will look good to everyone but our spouse.

Since children are accustomed to taking and taking, they do not see the destructiveness in the game until it is too late. Then they blame themselves.

You have seen "Daddy's little girl" all dressed up in her Easter dress with her little patent leather shoes hugging and kissing Daddy. You have seen a little boy pushing his dad away from his mom telling him "She's *my* mommy." Most parents think that this is just being cute and laugh at it. The laughter lets the child know that it is

OK, and so the game continues, and is reinforced.

If parents manage to stay together for longer than six years after a child is born, they then have the issue of sexuality to deal with. Children come into their sexuality between two and six. Yes, we said two and six. Just watch little ones play and you will see this for yourself.

Since most parents have judgements about sexuality, and since most people have never even acknowledged to themselves that they are sexual creatures, the issue goes ignored until the teen years. In the meantime, the children are misusing sexual energy. Because they do not know how to use it appropriately, it gets given to Mom or Dad. Children learn early how to use this energy to get what they want by watching Mom and Dad be uncomfortable with it.

Since it is never discussed, they continue to use it to manipulate and dominate the family into getting what they want. They use it more and more as they grow older. By this time, they are sure that using their sexual energy will get them what they want and so they use it more and more, indiscriminately.

Just look at the ten to twelve year olds of today. They are definitely sexual creatures. At what point does it become "not alright" for a little girl to sit on Daddy's lap? The answer is, when she begins to give her sexual energy to him and he starts to become uncomfortable about it. This can happen at any age. He does nothing about it, because good fathers are not supposed to have those feelings about their children. They are supposed to be "controlled." He begins to withdraw from her, and the more he withdraws, the stronger the child will come on with the energy. Children have been taught, through our own ignorance of the behavior, that this is one way to get what they want, quickly. The more the parent withdraws, the more the child comes on. Then there is a big upset and she feels totally rejected and then will not want to have anything to do with him. Alternatively, he may act out the energy by sexually abusing her. Then, she and the whole family can make him wrong and not have anything to do with him.

Little boys do it the same way, only they usually end up sleeping in the same bed with Mom and Dad, right in the middle.

One of the biggest mistakes we make is to believe that children do not have anything to do with what is going on in our relationship with our spouse — when all the time, due to the stand they took, they are engaged in a battle, with the result often being divorce or separation.

God gave us our children as a means to heal our family relationships with our parents, spouses and siblings. All children want is to be loved, nurtured and respected. All they want is to make a contribution to our families and know that they are an important contribution to us all. They want their home to be a warm, loving environment. They have not been properly managed to produce that result. The stands that they took have gotten the best of them. To avoid this, you must communicate with your children.

So that you are not fighting with your spouse about your children, and are being responsible for managing them, we recommend that you do the following: Give them duties that they pick, which are their contribution to the family. If they do not want to do anything, give them a choice of two. Let them select which one they will be doing.

We also recommend that you have family meetings in which, as a family, you make the house rules and consequences for not keeping the rules. If you are not willing to enforce the consequences, do not accept them as consequences. Children will make consequences ten times as harsh as parents would. If they choose a consequence that you cannot enforce, do not accept it as one.

People often say, "Well, why should we have to have rules? Our home is a democracy." Fiddlefoo. If this were true, there would be no upsetting events in families. There are things that go on in your home that are not OK with you. Unless you want to spend your life with your children fighting with them over the rules, you need to make the rules clear to your children, and ask them to determine the consequence if the rule is broken. Once the rules are established, post them on the refrigerator or somewhere else where they can be used for reference.

Kids want to be responsible. All we have to do is to teach them what we have learned (most of us through the "hard knocks of life") about actions and the consequences of their actions. In other words, teach them responsibility.

Most children would be thrilled to have this kind of a structure in their home. At least they would know, daily, what the rules are and would be certain that they were not going to change with the parents' mood swings and other random events. They could be responsible for following the rules or paying the consequences. It gives children the power that they need while structuring it to succeed for the family as a whole.

Many things can be done to produce harmony in the household which structure your children's lives to be bearable during those "unbearable" years.

1.   Communicate with your children about the sexual energy that is present in them. Let them know that their energy does not belong with you and your spouse. Let them know also that your spouse is the

only one you will be giving your sexual energy to. They will know what you are talking about. Their job is to see to it that you and your spouse remain in love with each other, or they do not get to be around you. They may test you for a while, but if you keep being true to your relationship with your spouse, they will quickly learn that it will not work anymore and the game will be ended.

2. When you cannot get your kids to pick up after themselves and you are ready to scream, we recommend that you start what we call a Saturday Box. This is a box for anything that gets left lying around where it doesn't belong. No one can take anything out of the box until Saturday. Friday evenings you will probably notice more things being left around, but once the kids see that you are putting anything you have to pick up in the box until Saturday, they will start being responsible for where they leave their things. This makes everyone, including Mom and Dad, responsible for where they put their things.

When we did this, our son loved to put our things in the Saturday box. It was frustrating at first; homework, books, everything went in the box and could not be taken out until Saturday. It took a few weeks to get adjusted, but soon the box became almost obsolete. We all became responsible for our things and did not have to fight to get our home in order.

3. Your children's job is to be sure that you are in good shape together. If the two of you are fighting, we recommend that the children be sent to another room until you are in good shape again. They will not want to go to their rooms, so they will be sure to get their job done by supporting your relationship.

4.   Divorce your children. Loosen and let go of the hold you have on them and the hold they have on you. Most people are so wrapped up in their children that they ignore their spouses. Make your spouse number one in your life and your children will take care of themselves. This allows you *both* to love them instead of just one of you.

The most important thing you can do with children is to communicate responsibly with them. This allows them to communicate responsibly with you.

Remember, you are the couple they are modeling their futures after. All you can teach them to do is to tell the truth about what they think, how they feel, and what they want in their young lives.

When you have successfully dealt with your family and your feelings, dealing with your children's feelings is a rich, rewarding experience.

Children are really a blessing to our lives and they need to know that they count, that they make a difference, and that they are loved. The only way to demonstrate this is to be consistent with your word, so they can be consistent with their word to you and themselves.

PARENTAL DISAPPROVAL SYNDROME

We can easily remember how we felt when we were children. All we have to do is to be with children and observe what happens in their everyday lives. When we were children we felt that our parents treated us harshly and sometimes we got angry with them. Being smaller than they, we could not express our anger to them, so we swallowed our feelings and our hurt. These feelings stay in our bodies until we grow up and become parents. The unresolved anger we had towards our parents then expresses itself to our children. If we have a stand to do things just the opposite from our parents, we may take it out on our spouse and withdraw from our children, for fear that we will hurt them.

Anytime we are extremely angry or enraged, we can know that it is not about the present situation. Such a strong emotion can rarely be generated in such a short period of time. Such emotions have usually been stored for some time until we blow up without even knowing what is happening.

The source of our upset usually relates back to a time with our parents when we wanted something and didn't get it, or felt taken advantage of, or felt taken for granted, or felt powerless in some way. Remember that any time you feel powerless in any situation, it is because *you* have given your power away. Look to see where you have given your power and be responsible for the occurrence.

Should you find yourself acting out your anger about your parents at your children, just communicate it to your kids; kids are the quickest to forgive and forget. Then you can forgive yourself. You deserve it. You are good parents!

FAMILY ORDER

Notice how our children seem to change when a new child enters our family. This often happens around age two, and so we think it is the source of the "terrible twos."

When the first child — a girl, say — is born into a family she is considered the star of the family. Everyone is thrilled at her presence. She is independent and rules the family . . . until the next child — a boy, say — comes along.

The first child is then replaced in her own mind as number one in the family, and is very upset. The conversation goes something like, "What's the matter, am I not enough for them? Am I not good enough?" She then takes a stand, that she is not good enough, and tries to dominate the family to win back the spotlight. She shuts down her feelings and will not allow anyone in as she says, "Well, if you don't want me, you won't have me." Looking at the so-called "terrible twos," you can see what we are talking about.

The second-born in the family, when the same sex as the first-born, generally takes a stand that they aren't good enough because they are the wrong sex (the ideal family in this country being one boy and one girl). This child grows up proving the stand that they aren't good enough.

Along enters child number three, usually after two years, or in whatever the family pattern has become by this time. The same scenario is then repeated with the other children.

You can see how important it is to communicate to your children and to remember what it is like to be a child and feel like a child. Children are very sensitive emotionally. Communication is the most important thing that will keep them open emotionally.

All of these characteristics are, in part, responsible for the recurring upsets that most families have. By communicating, being responsible for and completing our stands and judgements, we can save our selves, our children, and our families a lot of upsetting times.

BIRTH CHARACTERISTICS

The way children are delivered has a significant impact on the way they are in life. Some of these characteristics are:

1. Caesarian babies: These babies grow up to have a pattern of not completing things. They will start things and have big upsets so that someone will have to come and help them finish what they started, at the last minute. Very often these children will cut or injure themselves a lot.

2. Forceps deliveries: The above is also true for forceps deliveries. These children will have, more than usual, injuries to the head. There is also a pattern of headaches.

3. Breech birth: These babies seem to have a tough time getting along in life. Life is a struggle for them, as was their birth. Anger is a pattern in their lives, and they seem to have a difficult time getting along with others.

4. Anesthesia babies: These babies go unconscious a lot. They can grow up to be alcohol and drug users as they try to regain that feeling of the way it was when they were born.

5. Premature births: Premature babies are always in a hurry. They often feel rushed for time. The frequent feeling of being boxed in comes from the incubator which supported the beginning of their lives.

6.   Twins: Twins generally have upsets about being abandoned. They often have judgements about the one who came out first as being more loved. They make good partners.

Children are here to enjoy and love. So are we all.

*To be in the Kingdom is
to merely focus your full
attention on it.   T, 108*

CHAPTER 8

RELATIONSHIPS

We have discovered much that has assisted us in alivening our relationship, and in alivening the relationships of those with whom we have had the honor to work. Our commitment, through our work, is for people to have their relationships be more open, loving and satisfying. All people really want in a relationship is to be loved and nurtured by their partner. Everyone wants to feel like they are Number One in someone's life. Yet, what keeps occurring is a sequence of upsets.

Our first relationships are with our parents. We loved and lived with our parents and learned a great deal about how to be in relationship, by copying the way they were with each other. As we have said before, the way we demonstrate our love for our partner is the way we watched our parents interacting. This is not always the way that our partner demonstrates their love for us. They have different parents, who expressed their love differently.

If these two ways of expressing our love are not in agreement with each other, the outcome will be an upset and a feeling of not being loved.

To establish a working relationship with your partner, communicate how each of your parents demonstrated their love for each other. Then compare the ways of receiving love.

This will let your spouse know how you expect to receive love, thus giving them the opportunity to give love in the manner acceptable to you. It will also give you a clearer way to acceptably express your love for your partner.

In the process of relationship, it is very important to be in communication with each other, and to ask for what each of you wants. Some people have judgements about asking for what they want. Some think that they will not get what they want if they ask for it, so they don't bother. Your partner will be thrilled to know exactly what you want — it will keep them from guessing. If they don't give it to you, have that be OK, too, and acknowledge yourself for asking for what you want.

The way that most relationships start is that we meet someone and fall in love with them. They then become the "one," or our "king" or "queen." We have a marvelous time being with them; sex is great, conversation is great, time spent together or alone is great, and we enjoy spending more and more time together.

The more we are together, the more we want to be together, so we get married. Everything is wonderful . . . until we re-activate our cycle and our pattern. Suddenly, "He doesn't love me — He's not the one — Maybe I made a mistake — I should have listened to my mother" starts to dominate the conversations in your head. Our prince, at this point, turns into a big green frog. Ugh!

When we are in relationship, every time we reach our cycle (two years, or whatever our cycle is), we automatically start an upsetting event with our partner, as if they are the problem and it is their fault that we are having this upset. Have you ever noticed that it is always their fault? Or that it is your fault for picking the *wrong one*?

At the time that our pattern begins, we begin living from our head rather than our heart. If our partner is trying to let us know how much they love us, it is very frustrating, because our heart is so shut down (just as it was during the initial event), that we seldom allow ourselves to experience how much we are being loved in the process. Eventually, most partners give up at this point in trying to convince us how much they love us. More upset follows.

This gives us more evidence to make our stand right. "See, he really did not love me."

At this point the anger builds up between the two and there is no telling what will happen, except that communication in the relationship will cease.

RESPONSIBILITY

When communication ceases, one of the parties must be committed to rekindling the communication. Lack of communication comes from a fear of being hurt. When you are in touch with your love, it is natural to communicate responsibly.

The argument then comes up "which one?" Which one will step outside of their mind to discover that they are not upset about what they think they are upset about? Anger and rage are suppressed emotions. When they cause the kind of relationship damage that we are speaking of here, they can only be from past disappointments, hurts, etc.

So many times we have heard people say, "Well, I'm responsible, but so is she. Let her start first."

We have not met a couple yet who shared a fifty/fifty relationship that was as alive, joyous or spontaneous as it could have been. When you have a fifty/fifty relationship you always have the option of having the other person be responsible for your upset. When you make someone else responsible, you give them your power, which leaves you powerless to alter the situation.

When people are 100% responsible for their relationships, the relationship is viable. This means that they are willing to give up their attitude first and be "wrong" if necessary, in order to maintain the relationship. We are not speaking of submission (giving up), we are speaking of surrender (letting go).

When you are 100% responsible for your relationship, there is no one to blame for the way things are. You are responsible for the way things are in your relationship and as such, you begin considering why you perceive your partner the way you do. What are you being right about? What pattern is in play in the situation? What do you want that you didn't ask for? What is the communication that you need to make to have your relationship show up as whole and complete and in love?

You can see that only by owning *your* relationship can you possibly have a chance at living "happily ever after"? With the patterns, cycles, judgements and all the rest that our mind invents to keep us separate, it is not surprising relationships get into so many difficulties. When you are fully responsible for your relationship, magic can and does happen.

Most of us have one foot out the door before we enter into matrimony.

We often hear people say, "Well, if it doesn't work out we'll . . . ." In a relationship that is 100% responsible, there is no such thing as "if." The commitment in such a relationship is "our relationship is working and we are working our relationship." Both partners have a commitment to uncovering all the considerations they have about being in a committed relationship.

We, Barbara and Glenn, were in relationship for three years before getting engaged to one another. We played the game called "Well, if it doesn't work out . . . ." Our engagement lasted three weeks. We were so upset with each other and so upset with our thoughts about what marriage meant (tied down, just the word brings chills to most of us), that we gave ourselves one year to work out all the judgements we had made throughout our lives about how relationships didn't and couldn't work. After a year of continually communicating with each other and opening our hearts to discover what the true meaning of matrimony was, we again got engaged. We were married the following year. It was obvious to us both that we had made up a lot about the marriages that we had surrounded ourselves with. It was also clear that it did not have to be that way if we used what we knew, and lived our commitment to be 100% responsible for our relationship. We do.

COMMITMENT

One of the biggest fears about being in relationship is the fear of commitment. When we first started our relationship, we could only bring ourselves to be committed for one week at a time. We made each other the "King and Queen" for a week. At the end of that week we evaluated our relationship and renewed our commitment for another week. When we finally felt safe with a week long commitment, we then extended our commitment to a month at a time. After our month-long commitment, we then made a six-month commitment and made each other the one for six months. It felt much safer to re-commit each time, and it was not long before we made our life-long commitment and got married. By our wedding day, there was no doubt or question about whether or not we should commit ourselves to each other. Most people do not trust themselves to carry through on commitments and so they never make any. This procedure, of committing one week or month at a time, allows us to prove ourselves trustworthy to keep our commitments. If your fear of commitment has been keeping you from having a satisfying relationship, you might try the short-term commitment to complete that fear.

ALTERNATIVES

As we said, most people have one foot out the door before they enter into any relationship. They are afraid their stand — that they are not wanted — will come true at some point. The fact is, not a lot of people getting married these days are committed to being together *no matter what* happens. There is often a "what if."

We call these "what if's" alternatives. Most of us have something — divorce, separation, an affair or leaving of some kind — as an alternative to confronting what being in a relationship brings up.

When you are in a relationship or in love, you must expect things to come up. Love brings up anything unlike itself. It brings up your fears, doubts, worries, uncertainties, incompletions of the past, and stands. Love is the healing force. Be prepared to be healed of all negatives in your life and to fall in love.

We can be uncomfortable for a bit while we are working out our judgements about relationships, or we can keep our hearts closed and live like zombies. The choice is ours. People cannot exist for long without love, so eventually we are all likely to be in love with someone at some time in our lives.

When we have an alternative, other than resolving our judgements about our relationships, we are really giving our minds a back door which *will* be used at some time or another. Any alternative that you presently have in your relationship you will find a way to use. We cannot express this strongly enough. If we have an alternative of leaving, we will pull in any circumstance at the time of our pattern to justify our leaving. This way we don't have to face the issues which surface during our cycles.

When you have no alternative, you have no other choice but to stay and deal with the issue, unless you ignore it and hope it goes away for the next 50-75 years. Since most of us do not want to suffer for that length of time, we quickly resolve the issue, complete it and fall back in love with our "King or Queen."

It is powerful and freeing to close off the alternatives. When you have no alternative and your mind knows that you are staying with your partner no matter what is conjured up, all the conversations about "is he the one or isn't he" cease. All that is left is a peaceful certainty that no matter what, this is it for us. You will be amazed after you have taken that stand, to discover how much energy you used to use in questioning your choice in mates.

INTEGRITY

Integrity in our relationships is one of the most important qualities necessary to having and building a satisfying, trusting relationship. By integrity, we mean keeping our word and doing what we said we were going to do, and doing it when we said we were going to do it.

When we are not in integrity with our relationship (had an affair, etc.) we pay ourselves back immediately within three days. The way that we pay ourselves back is by having upsetting circumstances, such as our car breaking down, someone stealing something from us, or an accident or injury of some kind. Whenever these circumstances happen to us, if we look back to three days prior to the incident and find out where we were out of integrity, we will find the source of the upsetting event. We have punished ourselves for doing something that we say is wrong or shouldn't have been done.

We recommend you trust that your mate will be in integrity with the relationship. Trust is a gift that you give; it is neither earned nor deserved. It is a gift. So give the gift, especially if you have never trusted anyone before.

Know that as "when you take a stand everything comes up to prove you wrong about your stand," the same thing will happen when you give the gift of trust.

People may show up as being untrustworthy to you. All you can do is give the gift of trust again and keep looking for evidence that they are trustworthy. Eventually, they will show up as you say — trustworthy.

SEEING OURSELVES

It would be very hard for us to "see ourselves" or tell what it was that we are really upset about while we are in the midst of all our emotions about the upset. Since most people resist being told what to do or how to be, we also do not listen to our partners when they tell us how they feel we are being.

People call us and say, "My husband say's I'm not listening to him. What should I do?" We tell them to listen to him with their heart, not their head. How simple! It only *seems* complicated when you are engaged in the emotions of your upset.

When you give your partner permission to tell you the truth about what he sees about you when you are upset, and you can give him the trust it takes to make him right, no matter how your ego gets bruised, you can begin to see what is really upsetting you.

You have to consider that your partner is really committed to your being happy, joyful and excited. Your partner hurts when you hurt. He cries inside when you cry outside. He is committed to you being the best of all that you can be, regardless of all your judgements about him. Your partner would not be in relationship with you if there was not a deep caring and concern.

All you need give up in order to have your relationship work are your ego and righteousness. Then surrender into a more loving, positive, trusting relationship.

Ask for what you want and surrender your life to your relationship by cutting off any alternatives. You then begin living your relationship as the privilege that it is.

Being in a relationship is the most joyous, ecstatic and freeing feeling in the world when you can surrender your life to it and allow yourself to be in love.

Love heals all and love is all we ever need to be alive. Fully Alive!

SURRENDER VS. SUBMISSION

Since we have mentioned surrender and submission, we must now draw a distinction between the two.

A difference between submission and surrender is motivation. Submission is motivated by a desire to avoid an unpleasant future, e.g., peace at any price. Surrender is giving up the illusion of security created by negative patterns for the desire for something better.

Submission is often confused with surrender, as our interpretation of the words, is "giving in" to another. Submission, by our definition, is giving our power to someone else's authority, whereby they become responsible for the results that are produced, and we become the victim.

Surrender is bringing our power to someone else's power. We become responsible for them producing the result with us, and both of us are left powerful.

Submission, as all else, was learned at a young age. We wanted to play with the boy down the street and Mom didn't want us to. We said fine, we won't, and as soon as we left the house we did what we wanted to . . . visited the boy down the street. We gave our parents our power due to their authority (and size), until we left their physical presence. As soon as we were not around them, we pulled our power back — we couldn't exist without our power. This disempowered them and at the same time betrayed them (lying).

When we submitted to our parents, they became fully responsible for us and we became the victims of their authority. We could make them wrong for the way our lives turned out and we could be right that they did not love us.

Surrendering is bringing your power to someone else's power to produce a positive result. So, if we were to surrender to our parents in the above instance, we would see that our parents were concerned about the friends we were choosing. We would empower them to point out to us and teach us what we did not yet understand about peer pressure or whatever they were concerned about. They would be left empowered and so would we.

Surrender always leaves you empowered, and submission leaves you drained or feeling less than whole.

Our fear of surrendering is the fear that we will have to give up our power to someone else's authority the way we did with our parents, and we don't want to do that because of the upsets it caused in our family.

Submission *always* ends in betrayal. However it was that you betrayed your family, you will betray any organization that you are associated with until you complete your betrayal of your family.

This means to own it, complete it, communicate it and forgive yourself for it. Then take a new stand about surrendering vs. submitting.

Surrendering in a relationship is *the* most powerful thing that could move a relationship forward. Surrendering means that two equal partners are working together to produce the same result — love — and both are committed to the other one winning in all situations. As you can see, magic can come from that kind of a relationship.

Any time you are feeling taken advantage of or taken for granted, look to see if you are truly surrendering or if you are submitting to get approval or to avoid disapproval.

If you are submitting, shift to surrender. It is that easy. Poof.

Being in relationship will be more fun, spontaneous, alivened, and peaceful, if you do nothing more than just surrender.

Teach only Love,
For that is what you are.
T,87

CHAPTER 9

FORGIVENESS

So far our focus has been on how we took a stand and gave our word, which had the circumstances in our life show up the way that they did in a re-occurring time cycle. This was acted out in a pattern over and over. We have made judgements and evaluations about everyone and everything, which we get to be right about in order to have evidence that our stand is right.

In becoming conscious of the way that our minds work in relation to our daily affairs, we can begin to understand how powerful our word is, how powerful our emotions are and how powerful *we* are! When we can hold ourselves responsible for the outcome of the situations in our lives, we become the source of our circumstances. This ends our feelings of being helpless and victimized. We are the source of the events in our lives, whether we choose to believe this or not. That is simply the truth. The quicker we wake up and own that fact — whether we like it or not — the more power we will have to alter our world and the negative things in our world.

Some of us have done lots and lots of things to get better, to make our lives different but since we have not shifted our stand or completed our patterns, eventually the circumstances recur. Some of us have even given up on ourselves and have lost hope of life ever being any different from the way it is now.

There is no need for loss of hope in any situation unless you choose to give up on yourself. There are ways that we can impact the original stand that we took and complete it. We have already mentioned many, and here we would like to share some other techniques that have proven very powerful in completing our original stand.

CONSCIOUS BREATHING

For eight years we have been participating in guiding people in breathing sessions and training people to guide others in these breathing sessions, known as "Rebirthing Sessions." These sessions were developed by a man named Leonard Orr from Sierraville, California. These breathing sessions are the most powerful tool we have found to clear out the significant stands that we took at conception, in the womb, at childbirth, or early in our childhood.

These breathing sessions are even more powerful than the regressions that we spoke of earlier in the book and are recommended to all who have been born, regardless of the circumstances of your birth. As we said before, if you were born, you have a birth incident that can be cleared through conscious breathing.

There are some extremely well-written books that describe the process of rebirthing; we have listed them in the recommended reading section of this book and we suggest that you purchase them to discover more about the process. Permit us to give a very short description of the breathing process for your immediate understanding. We have the conviction that you will be interested enough to find out more about it.

Rebirthing is led by a professional rebirther who is committed to our completing our birth trauma or any events surrounding our birth. The rebirther will guide our breathing in such a way that there is no pause in our breathing. As we pull on the inhale of the breath we are taking in life forces, and as we relax on our exhale, we are clearing out whatever experience we have stored. These may be memories and pictures of the past, physical sensations, spiritual experiences or emotional releases. Whatever we need to release at the time will be released during our rebirthing session. A minimum of ten sessions are recommended to clear out whatever stand we have stored about our birth or related events.

Rebirthing is being done all over the world, as millions of conscious breathers celebrate the breath of life, increased vitality and aliveness.

Rebirthers are special people who are well trained and committed to assisting you in completing your past.

While there are thousands of experiences we could share with you about the people we have rebirthed, we will relate only one.

A woman to whom we had introduced rebirthing and trained as a professional rebirther related this experience she had with her grandson. Her grandson was failing the second grade for the second time. He was hyperactive and could not get along with anyone, including his teachers, principal or mom. This woman asked her daughter if she could rebirth her grandson. Her daughter said, "Sure, Mom, do anything!" as she was frustrated at her son's behavior. The grandmother asked her grandson if he would like to do a breathing session with her and he said he would.

The session began with him lying down with his eyes closed as his grandmother began guiding him in his breathing. After about ten minutes of breathing she asked him what was happening. His reply was, "My fingers and toes are tingling like they have been asleep." After a while, she asked again and he replied, "My mouth is numb like I've been to the dentist." As he continued breathing she again asked what was happening, and he told her, "I'm not out yet." As the session continued, she again asked him what was happening and he replied, "My head is right there!", as he was experiencing crowning at his birth. He continued to breath and she again asked and his response was, "I can not believe it, Grandma, I am half in and half out!" As the session continued he said, "I am lying on a table and the doctor is wiping the blood off of me. But Grandma, why did he have to hit me so hard? I didn't do anything." A while longer she asked him what he was going to do next. His reply was, "They are going to put me in that glass box over there!! My mother is going to let them take me away from her and put me in that glass box over there!" He was so angry when he said this that it startled his grandmother for a moment and he cried like a newborn. He had been angry his entire childhood about being taken away from his mother and put in an incubator. He blamed his mother for letting the doctors do this to him, and he had never forgiven her. His grandmother asked him, "Do you know how to forgive your mother?" He replied, "No," so she told him that his mother did not know that he would be so angry about being put in an incubator or she would never have let them do that to him. She then asked him if he could let it be OK with him now. He told her that he could and that it was OK with him now. He breathed a while longer and completed his session.

Within two weeks, he was getting 100% on his spelling tests. His anger, hyperactivity and rebelliousness were gone, and he started getting along well with everyone. His mom was able to remarry and the family moved to another town. A year later when his grandmother came to visit, this little boy was showing her his good third grade papers. He told her, "These good papers are because we did that thing together. Remember, Grandma?" He had forgiven his mother, let it be alright that he had been placed in an incubator, and healed his relationships with everyone after just one session of rebirthing.

All of us have an event that we took a stand on that is running our lives as much as it was this little boy's. Most of us don't remember what the event was. Rebirthing is a tool we can use to recall, recreate and complete that event.

It is time for us all to clear out our past traumas and start fresh with a new and powerful stand about our lives.

AFFIRMATIONS FOR CLEARING

Affirmations are statements that we tell ourselves daily that effect our experience of how we see the world. They can be positive or negative. They produce the result according to whatever you are saying about your world. The original stand that we took was an affirmation that, as we have seen, has had a tremendous impact on our life. If you are going to use affirmations, and we highly recommend that you do, be sure to speak your affirmations with the power of any intense emotion. What cements an affirmation is saying it in the midst of the emotion. Remember that you can use *any* emotion: Love, praise and gratitude, or anger, fear, and hatred.

In the Alivening Weekends we facilitate, we present a series of forgiveness affirmations designed to free us from upsetting judgements and evaluations that we made when we were born. These forgiveness affirmations were developed by using a process of muscle testing, known as Psycho-Kinesiology, to determine which statements had the most impact on the most people. Here are some of the most frequently used affirmations: "I now completely forgive my parents for wanting me to be a boy (or a girl)." "I now completely forgive myself for resenting my parents for wanting me to be a boy (or a girl)." We have recorded these affirmations on cassettes to assist you in freeing yourself from your negative stands taken during birth. See the Recommended Reading List for details.

PRAYER POWER

Prayer is one of the most positive ways to affirm your desired good. There is a drawback, in that most people think of prayer in terms of religion. This is not what we are talking about. We are speaking about talking directly to God, whoever or whatever that is to you and opening your heart to Him/Her to ask for assistance and guidance.

When we are open and vulnerable, we have a direct connection to God, since He/She resides in our hearts. The power of our spiritual connection is all we ever need to resolve any and all situations. We must open our hearts to receive guidance and assistance, and we must ask for what we want.

When we open our hearts and generate the feelings of love, praise and gratitude to thank God for all that has been given to us, and we ask for forgiveness for those areas of our life that we have been unable or unwilling to forgive ourselves for, a peacefulness washes over us and engulfs us. If God feels that we are worth forgiving, we must be! Everything else melts away. Forgiveness is the healing balm of love!!

In any situation that you feel you cannot resolve, if you would just open your heart and allow yourself to forgive or be forgiven, God's love will wash away all your troubles.

Forgiveness affirmations, when delivered with all the intensity of love, praise and gratitude, free all who are involved to be who they are. A direct link is established between the forgiver and the forgivee in this interaction. Love becomes their link.

To accept your littleness
is arrogant, because it means
that you believe your
evaluation is truer than God's.
                    T, 167

CHAPTER 10

MONEY

Money acts the way it does in our life as a result of the stand we took about it in the midst of an upsetting event involving money. The stand we have about money makes us right about the stand we have about our life, which is usually taken when we are young. If our parents felt that they could not afford to have a baby and were arguing about this issue when we were in the womb we may have money tied into our self worth.

Some people do not take stands about money until later in their childhood. One person discovered his stand was taken when as a young boy he took money from the collection plate at church. He did not get caught and felt guilty for having stolen from "God." His stand about money was that he did not deserve to have any. After having stolen the money from the church, he had to spend it quickly on items that could not be seen, otherwise, everyone would have asked him where he got it from and would know that he stole it. He spent the money on food and drinks and other things that he could enjoy without leaving any trace.

His financial life followed suit thereafter. He would make large sums of money and spend it on things that no one could see: fine dining, expensive hotels, lavish gifts for his girlfriend and friends and other things. He had essentially no assets for his own personal use. He was still guilty about having stolen money and could not allow himself to have anything to show for his money.

After telling the truth about his out integrity with the church, and discovering his stand about money, he completed his stand about money and after just two weeks doubled his income.

Everyone has a time in their life when they felt out of integrity with money. They either stole money from their parents or siblings, took candy from the store, took money from pockets during gym class, or did something to make themselves feel that when it came to money, they were thieves.

Their relationship with money, thereafter, was that they were guilty and their stand was they didn't deserve to have any. If they got caught, they were punished, humiliated and felt guilty, which, for some, is when they took their stand about money. If they didn't get caught, they had the fear of being caught someday. They were guilty so they would punish themselves. This was happening as they took their stand. There is always some area in which people feel guilty about their relationship with money.

We have been punishing ourselves all our lives for our out integrities. We will not allow ourselves to prosper or be financially successful because we are afraid that we will be caught. We feel guilty spending money on ourselves because of our past out integrities. We use our stand about money and our judgements about ourselves for having done what we did to keep us from being the financially prosperous people that we are meant to be.

In order to allow ourselves to prosper and give ourselves permission to establish a healthy relationship with money we have designed the following process:

Since we have already judged ourselves guilty, let us pretend that we are in a court of law so that we can be complete with these money issues once and for all. You will be your own Judge, Jury and Jailer.

1. Make a list of all of your past out integrities with money: all the times you stole from someone, shoplifted, didn't pay parking tickets, lied to the Internal Revenue Service, or any time that you felt you stole something from someone. Take your time to do this list and write down as many times as you can remember that you judged yourself as a thief in some way.

2. Now you are your Judge and Jury. You plead guilty to all the charges. Write "guilty as charged" across your list.

3. Determine for yourself what amount of money will be your fine. The 30 days or $30 trial. In other words, you are fining yourself for all of your past misdoings with money so that by the time you are complete with this process, you will be squeaky clean with money issues from the past. Your fine should

be enough to make you feel as if you have been fined but not enough to take food off the table. You then pay that amount of money to any organization or persons who are supporting you in your spiritual growth. You give it as a gift to God.

4. Declare yourself complete with your past out integrities and with the stand that you have had in the past pertaining to money. Then declare a new stand about how money will operate for you in the future, with the intensity of an emotion.

Once you have done this, many more out integrities will be revealed to you. When you start thinking about them, just remember that your past with money is now complete and you can no longer use that to invalidate yourself or hold yourself back.

Someone came to us in upset about his job. He was either going to get fired from his job or was going to quit. He had many negative judgements about his boss, clients, and coworkers. We told him to do the above process and then communicate all of his judgements to his boss and be responsible in his communication for the way things were. He followed our advice and completed the process. In the midst of the process he took a new stand about money. He went back to his boss and communicated all of his judgements responsibly, and instead of getting fired was given a ten thousand dollar a year raise. He was certainly in ecstasy when he shared this miracle with us!

What most of us use when we are looking for a reason to invalidate ourselves is money. When we are clean with money — in other words, when we give our word about our financial affairs and we keep our word — we have no evidence to use to invalidate ourselves.

We recommend that you make a list of everyone that you owe money to and pay them, or set up a payment plan that you can keep. It is important that you keep your word on this plan so you can establish yourself as trustworthy about money.

If others owe you money and they have not kept their agreements, write to them and give it as a gift. Know that what you freely give *will* come back to you multiplied! If you have not collected the money from them yet and it is causing hard feelings or ending a relationship, it cannot possibly be worth the emotional turmoil. How can we put a price on a human relationship? That is what we are doing when we end relationships over money. We are saying that $10,000, or however much money is owed, is worth more to us than the relationship we have with the person who owes us. How can we possibly put a price tag on one of God's creations?

Free yourself from someone owing you something so that you can collect what is yours from the universe. If you don't know how to contact them, write the letter to them and mail it in their name care of God with no return address. This will give you a feeling of completion and get it off your mind.

INCOME CEILING

Many people have a self imposed income ceiling that keeps them in the same income bracket no matter how hard they try to increase their income. This income ceiling is usually a little bit higher than our parents income was, adjusted for inflation. Our life style, however, is about the same as theirs was, or perhaps a little better than theirs. When we shared this with one group, a man said he didn't see where he had an income ceiling. Soon he saw the truth about his income ceiling, however, when he noticed that one year he had made ninety-five thousand dollars, and his father asked him his income for the year. He told his dad how much he had made and his dad's response was, "I never made that much in my whole life!" The very next year his income dropped to fourteen thousand dollars. He could see how he had adjusted his income to be more in line with his dad's income.

One of the reasons we have our income ceiling is so that our parents can give things to us. When we were young, our parents showed their love for us by showering us with gifts at holiday times or birthdays. If we are successful and have everything we want, then our parents cannot give us anything and we feel like we are not being loved by them, since most of us think of gift giving as a way of expressing love.

To discover what your income ceiling is, compare your annual income with your parent's annual income and see how close they are. Is your life style just a little bit better than theirs? If the self-imposed income ceiling is stopping you from having the income you desire and deserve, declare yourself complete with the stand you took about the amount of money you can make, and take a new stand on what you rightfully deserve.

PERSONAL LENDING

Very often family and friends have come to us to borrow money. In the past we would loan them the money. When they failed to keep their word about paying us back, we had a big upset with them and made them wrong about not keeping their word the way they said they would.

When we lend people money and they do not pay us back, we get to feel like we are better than they are. Our self-righteousness takes over. Instead of having our money back we would rather be able to keep them less than us, because they do not pay us back.

When people ask us to lend them money, and we feel they are presently unable to repay the loan, and we feel we want to assist them, we give them the money as a gift. We know that what we freely give comes back to us multiplied. This way, everyone wins and no one is less than the other.

TITHING

A most important thing that we have learned is to acknowledge God for the abundance that He/She provides for us daily. The way that we do this is through tithing.

Tithing is giving a percentage of our income back to God as an acknowledgement for the abundance He/She has brought to us. The first check that we write every month is to God. Since we have been doing this, we have not been concerned about having enough money. We consider God to be our financial consultant and whenever we need money, we just ask for it and it is there. It is not always in the ways that we expected it, but it is always there.

Whenever you feel that you cannot afford to tithe is the time when you need most to tithe. Certainly demonstrating your gratitude for having an overabundance of money in your life is necessary, when you believe that you do not have enough.

Again there are hundreds of books. We enjoy Catherine Ponder's books the best, because they are written from a spiritual context of giving our word, the power of our word and being open to receiving God's blessings.

Larry Dolan says it's not that we give God 10% and keep 90% but rather that God lets us use His/Her 90% and keeps 10% for Him/Her self.

Since we have been tithing, our income has doubled, our peace of mind quadrupled and the gratitude in our hearts spreads daily as we thank God for this paradise called life.

We realize that there is a lot of noise in your head about what we have or haven't said in this Chapter. We consider the topic of money as an ongoing process that can always be expanded upon. We have available our money seminar tape for those who wish to explore the process in more detail.

"Except you become as little children" means that unless you fully recognize your complete dependence on God, you cannot know the real power of the Son in his true relationship with the father.   T, 10

CHAPTER 11

LOVE, SEX, AND POWER

We purposely are writing about love, sex, and power in the same chapter because we know they are very sensitive areas in people's lives. They are personal and private for most of us and a taboo topic for some of us.

We want to point out a very important distinction at this time, a distinction that most people think they have made, but when they really listen with their hearts, see that they haven't. This is the distinction between love and sex.

Most of us believe that one equals the other: love equals sex or sex equals love, when really they are two entirely different things.

Sex is sex and love is love. It is not surprising that we have them collapsed, when we see where we first learned about sex.

We learned about sex when in the womb. Our parents were having sex and we were in there either cheering them on or in terror of being hurt and wanting them to stop. Thus, our decisions and stand about sex would be either "Go for it," or "Leave me alone."

We were clear that our parents loved each other when we were in the womb. Since they were having sex, sex must equal love. As we grew up, we wanted to feel loved, and decided that in order to be loved as much as our parents loved each other, sex had to be included. Since we decided that love equals sex, and we did not have sex with our parents, we felt unloved.

Some of us judge how much we are loved by how often we have sex. If we do not have sex a lot we must not be loved a lot.

We learn at a very early age about sexual energy and learn to use it to get what we want. This behavior is reinforced daily until we forget that we even have sexual energy. It is so much a part of us that we become unconscious of the fact that we are using it. Thus, we give it out indiscriminately to whomever happens to be around: the waitress, our parents, our best friend's husband, or whomever is around that we want approval or acceptance from.

The problem with this is that if we are in a committed relationship, we are exhausted from giving so much energy to everyone all day that we have none left for our mate.

We call the indiscriminate giving of our sexual energy "Snaking." When we can be responsible for the fact that we have sexual energy, we can begin to direct that energy towards empowering all areas of our relationship.

When we have not been responsible for something, we have no power to alter it. So far, we have been irresponsible for our sexuality. Thus, we have had no choice in how we use it. We can now be responsible and give our sexual energy to whom we choose, not just to anyone.

SENSUALITY VS. SEXUALITY

Since love equals sex to most of us, anything that is perceived as sensual will be thought of as sexual. Our mothers were very sensual with us when we were a child — gently stroking our hair, massaging our backs, and doing all the things that mothers do for babies. When we have sensuality and sexuality confused, it does not leave much room for gentle, nurturing work like massage or Rolfing, Postural Integration or Soma (deep tissue body work), because whenever some one is sensual with us we automatically think of sexual.

If you can begin to notice when you feel sensual that you turn it to sexual, you will be on the right path to discovering the difference between the two.

Again, it will take vigilance on your part to do this. It is not wrong to have love and sex combined or even to have sensuality and sexuality combined. It just limits your choice of reactions to certain situations in life. Anything that limits our choices is worth checking into.

COMMUNICATION

As we have said in the chapter on Relationships, integrity in our relationships can "make or break" a relationship. If we have given our sexual energy to someone else — the waitress, or our boss — the sexual energy we give to them *does* affect our relationship. If we have physically acted out this energy, had an affair with our secretary, every time that we are with our mate, guess how we feel? Guilty. The person we had the affair with is between us and our mate.

A young couple came to us for consultation. The young man was recuperating from having had a heart attack six weeks prior. During one process, the young man communicated to his wife that he had had an affair with someone else seven or so years *prior* to the consultation and apologized to her. After clearing her shock, she was able to listen to his apology, look for her responsibility in the matter and forgive him for his betrayal of her. Afterwards, he shared that for the first time in seven years, he could see her eyes clearly. When he had betrayed her, he could no longer look into her eyes for fear that she would see his betrayal.

He became very clear that he had kept his communication stored in his body until he "blew up his heart," and he knew that if he were to heal his heart condition, he would have to tell her the truth and take whatever consequences needed to heal their relationship, and thus his heart.

They healed their relationship; he lost weight and healed his heart; and they are more in love with each other than they have ever been before.

When we are out integrity in our relationships, we will pay ourselves back. For this young couple it took seven years of suffering through withheld communications. The quicker we are willing to communicate our betrayals, withholds and judgements, the quicker we can let go of them.

SOUVENIRS

Very often betrayals are prompted by the "souvenirs" we have lying around from other relationships. Just as we collect souvenirs from our vacations and trips abroad, so have we collected souvenirs from our past relationships. Some of us have souvenirs from the very first time we kissed, had sex, or went away together with someone. Every time that we see these souvenirs, our mind pulls in the memories of those times, some of which were good times and others not so good.

This may not be on a conscious level, since some of the souvenirs we have "saved" are so familiar to us that we do not even relate them consciously to any one memory.

Some of us are sleeping in the same bed with our "King or Queen" that we slept in with perhaps dozens of people. The result is upset in the bedroom. How can we be true to one person when we have gifts and souvenirs all around reminding us of "old what's-his-name."

Not only are we reminded of our previous relationships, but our mate is also reminded that we have had previous relationships. Certainly, most of us have, but why have things around to remind ourselves and our mate? By having old relationships lying around, constantly reminding us of a failed relationship or a painful relationship or whatever we said about it, the only choice we have is to make ourselves right that in relationships we are a failure, or that men hurt us or whatever? Having souvenirs lying around sets us up to fail by reminding us that we failed before.

Clean out all old relationships from your space! Get rid of anything and all things that are souvenirs. Give old pictures to your children if they want them, find new owners for the jewelry that was given by other lovers, get rid of all the furniture that was a part of someone else. What you freely give will come back to you multiplied. Create some room for your new and highest good to come back to you.

If our lives are so jammed with the past, how can we expect anything new to fit? It cannot, there is no room for it.

There is a universal law of vacuum which, stated simply, is that the universe abhors a vacuum. Where there is space, the universe will fill it. You get to choose what it gets filled with, and if you don't, the universe will.

Create a vacuum for yourself. What good you created for yourself once, you can create for yourself again. Make room for your new or transformed relationship to show up in. Every time that you find something that reminds you of a past relationship, get rid of it.

As you do this, you will be completing with your past relationships. You will be loosing and letting them go to their highest good as you are releasing and letting go of your past to your highest good. Forgive yourself and your past relationship for all ill feelings and be responsible for the messes you have made. You may need to be in communication to do this; it is up to you.

What is incomplete in your relationships is incomplete in your world!

That's a pretty strong statement. If you keep reminding yourself of that, you will keep holding yourself as responsible 100% for the condition of your relationships.

Set people in your past free. Set yourself free of your past. Declare your freedom.

WHAT WORKS

To have a successful sexual relationship, we suggest the following:

1. Make a commitment to master snaking (the using of your sexual energy inappropriately) and stop giving your energy to people other than your mate. When you catch yourself doing it, communicate it to your mate and return them back to their throne.

2. Keep your mate present with you when you are away from each other physically. Whenever you have sexual thoughts about someone else, think of your mate.

3. Ask your mate for what you want! Ask your mate to ask you for what they want, and give it to them. Keep communicating with each other with a commitment to serving each other 100%.

4. After asking for what you want, take what you get, even if it does not fit your pictures of what you wanted.

5. Clear out all past souvenirs and open your heart to your mate. Allow yourself to "fall madly in love" and see what happens.

POWER

When we are willing to be responsible for the results we have been producing thus far in our lives, we can see with certainty that we *are* powerful. Thinking that we are a victim of any circumstance, event or person leaves us powerless to alter the situation. We can see that everything we have done has been to serve us in making ourselves right about what we have said. We can see that everything that has happened to us has been absolutely perfect and has given us tremendous value and benefit. Each time we become responsible for an occurrence or event, we become more and more powerful. Power comes from our word taken in the midst of any emotion.

We are always using our power to produce a result, and for the most part only feel we are powerful if we like the result. Usually when we do not like the result we feel the victim of our circumstances and thus feel powerless.

Surrendering to a situation or circumstance that we do not like is the easiest way we know of to become powerful again. Once you have made the distinction between surrender and submission, it will become clear that when we are powerless, we have submitted to someone else's authority. When we surrender we are powerful because we have brought our power to someone else's power, thus increasing our power as well as theirs.

In knowing that everything that has happened in our life is the result of our giving of our word, we can begin to see the power that we are. When we can be responsible for the power that we are, we can begin to choose what we are going to bring forth powerfully in our lives. When we can powerfully choose what we are bringing forth in our lives, we can heal our planet.

So give your word with the intensity of the emotions and keep it. No matter what you have to do to keep your word, always do what you say you are going to do. Start to trust that you can keep your word. Stop invalidating yourself.

Power is nothing more than giving your word and keeping it. If you look at powerful people, you will see that the most important thing in their lives is that they are consistently in integrity with what they say. You can count on them to keep their word when they give it to you and you never doubt that they will. This allows you to bring your power to their power to have them produce the result.

Start validating the power that God has given you through your words and emotions. God wants us all to be powerful, alive and in love. Let's give Him/Her what He/She wants.

*Having rests on giving
and not on getting! T, 102*

CHAPTER 12

HEALTH

What relationship does our stand have with our health? What influence does it have? If we are truly powerful by our word and emotions, how can we relate this to our health?

Our body is designed to last over 900 years. Every seven years we have a whole new body, because daily our old cells are dying off and being replaced with new ones, with the exception of the brain cells which change at the molecular structural level. This being the case, why do we look and feel the way that we do? Because of the stand that we took about aging, illness and dis-ease, and because, thus far, we have not examined closely our beliefs in these areas.

Our body is the most marvelous miracle in the world. It is designed to regulate and take care of itself, and the one thing that keeps it from being successful at this, is the judgements we have about it. If you do not like your body, change your mind about it.

When our integrity is out with ourselves, we pay ourselves back, as we have said before. Most often this is a physical pay-back, through an accident, illness, etc. When people do not allow themselves to cry, they get a cold; when we do not allow ourselves to be supported, we get backaches, and on and on. Within three days of when our integrity is out, we have paid ourselves back. When we can discover the source, we can heal ourselves of our health problems.

A young couple came to us in a tremendous upset. They had just gotten engaged and while having the blood test done for the marriage license, the young man discovered he had leukemia. The doctors told him he had less than a year to live and to reconsider marriage. They went for a second opinion and heard the same diagnosis.

We arranged to have dinner with them to discuss the matter. At dinner he discovered the source of his dis-ease. He was Jewish and she was Christian, and his family was terribly upset that he was marrying outside of their faith. His mother told him that if he did this she would disown him as her son. He let her know that he was going to do it regardless of what she thought. She then told him that if he married outside of the faith he would have bad blood and to her he would be literally dead. She would not speak with him or be associated with him in any way. His leukemia, he found, was a result of making her right that he was now "bad blood" because of his choice in marrying his wife. He was also making his mother right that he was dead if he married her. When he discovered what he was doing to himself, he had a choice to not get married and heal himself or have a conversation with his family and have it be alright with them that he was marrying outside of the faith. He did the latter. He apologized for the things that he told his body about his blood and having to die to be right about what his mom said. He continued processing this and did affirmations daily for two weeks or so. When he returned to the doctor for his check up and another blood test was drawn, he had no leukemia. He went to another doctor for a second opinion and still had no leukemia. Within three days of having told the truth about what was dis-easing him, he had healed himself. They are now married and he has had no recurrence after a year.

Another couple came to us with their daughter. She had had several severe problems with her ears and doctors wanted to put tubes in her ears because the medication they were giving her was not working. Since tubes in the ears is a very common practice for nontreatable ear infections, no one thought the least of it. Her parents did not want her to suffer any longer, but they did not want her to have to undergo surgery, either. We suggested that they do a rebirthing session with the child, and they agreed to try, with little hope that rebirthing would do anything. While they were breathing the baby began to cry and after a while took up the connected breath that her parents were breathing. We told the baby while she was breathing that it was alright for mommy and daddy to fight. We told her that they loved each other and would be together always no matter how loud they screamed at each other, and that she did not have to injure her ears because she was frightened of hearing. She did nothing but continue to breathe. Her appointment to begin the operation was scheduled for three days after the session.

Her parents requested that she be checked prior to surgery to see if she still needed to have the surgery. When she did not, the doctors and her parents were shocked. Never again did they underestimate the power of a child. She has had no recurrence of ear problems since then, and it has been over three years. Every time they yell at each other they apologize, and they let her know it is OK and she doesn't have to stop hearing.

We have story upon story of how we can heal ourselves by first being responsible for making ourselves unwell in the first place. We are the source of all illness and all health. We think that we get a lot of attention for being ill. We think we get more love when we are ill. We think that we get more help when we are ill. We can have just as much love, nurturing and attention when we are well as we can when we are ill. We make ourselves ill when we feel unloved or uncared for, usually right in the cycle of our pattern.

The natural state of our bodies is *health*. Anything other than health is your body crying out for you to wake up and heal yourself of your negative thoughts or actions. When you clear your thoughts and actions, you can heal your body.

Listen to your body. It will tell you what it needs. Treat it like the miracle that it is and it will always do for you whatever you want it to. Stop giving it cold pricklies. Start telling it how wonderfully young, alive and healthy it is, and it will start responding to your every command.

Every seven years we have a whole new body so if we don't like the way that our body is now, we can, over a seven year period of time, have a whole new body or any part thereof that we dislike, since our cells are being replenished everyday.

We once had a married couple in our Weekend whose biggest problem was that he liked girls with round bottoms and she had a flat bottom. It was very upsetting to her because she was invalidating her bottom at every opportunity and it kept getting flatter and flatter. She felt she was not good enough for him because she had a flat bottom and he liked round bottoms. When she discovered that every day cells are being replenished, she decided to do something about her flat bottom other than just complain about it. She declared that she was going to have a round bottom within five days. He was in the navy and was going out to sea for five days. She declared that by the time he returned, she would have a nice round bottom. She went out and bought a Playboy magazine and picked out a picture of the bottom that she wanted hers to be like, nice and big and round. She cut it out and put it on her refrigerator and every day she would study it and tell herself, "That's what my bottom looks like now." Everyday, several times a day she examined that picture and declared her new bottom. Every time she thought about her bottom she pictured hers as being the one in the picture. When he came home from duty, they were in the shower together and he exclaimed, "Wow, what happened? You have a round bottom."

Our body aligns with our thinking. Think only the highest thoughts of love, praise and gratitude for the Gifts that God has given us. Give thanks for our health, our energy, our youthfulness, our eyesight, our hearing, our emotions, and our beautiful bodies. Any time that a cold prickly enters our thoughts we can immediately cancel it and apologize to our body for our cruelty to it and give thanks for the healthfulness of it. Every seven years we have a whole new body. If you don't like the way it is now, picture it the way you want it to be and you will become as your picture. Praise your body at every opportunity.

> *We will not let the beliefs of*
> *the world tell us that what God*
> *would have us do is impossible.*
> *Instead, we will try to recognize*
> *that only what God would have us*
> *do is possible.   W. 71*

CHAPTER 13

ACKNOWLEDGING YOUR DIVINITY

What we have presented so far in this book is that we gave our word in the midst of an emotional upset and that the circumstances of our lives have happened to make us right about what we said. The power of our word generated the events and people that we have experienced. We are 100% responsible for all that has happened to us, and we are not a victim of anything.

We gave our word with intensity and the power of our emotions, and our word became real in the world. What we said happened, and we became right about it.

That is the power that we are, that we could say how it would be and have the results show up making us right about what we said.

We have given our word in another area. We gave our word, we took a stand, and we live our life out of this stand as if it is the only way, and the stand that we took and live our life out of is, "death is inevitable!" With this stand what we get to be right about is that we have to die, and the natural result is dying. Our entire life is designed to bring us closer to death, as if we are the victim of God's cruel joke.

Our first experience of death is birth. We die to womb life and are born into the physical world. Our birth was traumatic for most of us. We resisted the pain and travail of our birth — our death to womb consciousness. What we resist persists. At around four years of age, the people we love the most begin to teach us that death is inevitable. Some of them even die to prove to us how right they are about their stand that death is in fact inevitable. By the time we are nine years of age we have enough evidence that death is inevitable to make it our stand, hook, line, and thinker. From then on everything we do brings us closer to our death.

What evidence do we use to prove that someone is dead? It used to be that when people would die, we would dig a shallow hole in the ground and place them in it, say a few words and then cover them up with dirt. Two to three days later they would wake up, dig their way out, and come walking back down the street. It scared people to have this going on, so they worked out several ways to keep people dead when they died. The ways we agreed on to keep people dead were to take out all their blood and fill them with formaldehyde, put them in a box and screw the lid down on it, place the box in a concrete vault, and bury the vault six feet under the earth. This would assure everyone that those who had died would stay dead. In some belief systems, all of this had to happen within twenty-four hours of the time the person died.

What is the measurement we use to determine when someone is dead? We know a man who reported that he had a heart attack and was pronounced dead on arrival at the hospital after showing no vital signs at all. The doctors at the hospital pronounced him dead, signed the death certificate, and sent his body to the hospital morgue. He came back to life six hours later while lying on a stretcher in front of the hospital morgue freezers. The only reason he wasn't in the freezer was because they were all full. He said he woke up, sat up, the sheet went flying, and so did the attendant. The doctor came running into the room and started pounding on his chest as if to revive him, but he was already back alive.

Who is it that we are, anyway? There is a photographic process developed by a Russian couple named Kirlean that photographs the energy around plants, animals, and humans. This energy body changes colors in humans depending on what thoughts we are having, what drugs we have taken, or what emotions we are experiencing. In photographing this energy body (known as the aura) around pregnant women they detected a colorful ball of energy in the mother's aura up near her head that was pulsating and vibrating. For the first twelve weeks of the baby's development the baby is not connected to the mother's systems at all. In regressions, many people have discovered that this colorful ball of energy is creating the baby's body during this time, placing the fingers, the eyes, the nose, the ears, determining the sex, and all other systems where they should be. When the fetus is fully formed, it is then hooked up through the placenta, and the mother's circulatory system begins to nourish the baby. During the birth process, that colorful ball of energy comes down from the mother's aura and penetrates into the baby in the area of the solar plexus. We then say the baby is alive. The baby stays alive, grows, and goes through life until it dies, at which time that colorful ball of energy withdraws from the body, leaving from the solar plexus, and goes back home. We then say that person is dead.

Other tests were done, placing people who were near death on beds that were resting on very sensitive scales. It was discovered that humans lose three quarters of an ounce in weight at the moment of death. Animals do not.

Who we are is a colorful ball of energy that weighs three quarters of an ounce and is inhabiting this physical body. Some people call this the soul.

All accidents, illness, injuries, etc., are the result of living our lives from the context that death is inevitable. These kinds of upsets lead us closer and closer to our death, making us right that we have to die. This happens in our pattern/time cycle. Just look back at your patterns and cycles and see how many are linked to physical unwellness. What if our stand, that death is inevitable, is a lie? What if we have been living a lie? What if dying is a result of us giving our word in the midst of an upset and making ourselves right about what we said? What if we have used the power of our word to create our own death?

PHYSICAL IMMORTALITY

Do you know anything in this world that has no opposite? Up or down, black or white, day or night? What is the opposite of death? If we are powerful enough to give our word as infants and have what we said made real in the world, we are powerful enough to proclaim death is inevitable and have that result produced. We can take a different stand that we will be right about, that would bring us more alive. We can take the stand, in the midst of intense emotion, that "physical immortality is a reality!" The natural result that we produce is *alivening*; everything we do would contribute to our aliveness and the aliveness of others, or we wouldn't do it. Within this stand we would have "youthing" instead of aging, until we reach the age we want to maintain and then we would have agelessness. We would be healthy instead of being sick, we would have energy instead of being tired, and we would be safe in the world. It is unsafe living in a world where death is inevitable, because we are always waiting for "the death blow" to strike. We never fully open our hearts to love anyone because we know they will die and we will be hurt when they do.

This does not mean it is wrong to die. It means you have a choice in the matter. Most people spend their lives clearing their birth trauma so they can die and start all over by being born again, go through life clearing their birth trauma then die, over and over. We call this the cycle of reincarnation and karma.

Our body is designed to last for over nine hundred years. With nine hundred years to live, do you think we have enough time to do all we want to do? Every seven years we have a whole new body. We can have our body be healthy, energetic, and alive by declaring our immortality. We can be safe in the world. We can open our hearts to fully love our mate, knowing that they do not have to die. Our word, given with intensity, makes our reality. How will we have it? The fountain of youth rests between our ears, not in some far off distant place.

OUR DEATH

Through progressions, we have discovered that out
of our strong commitment to death — our stand that death
is inevitable — we have already set up the circumstances
of our death. We have determined the age we will die, the
clothes we will be wearing, the events that are taking
place, the people who are involved, and everything else
involved in our death. We even know what our lesson was
in this lifetime. We are not the victims of our death, we
are the source of it. We have the cast of characters
already lined up to participate in the drama of our death.
"All Death Is Suicide!"

As theorized in Psychorientology, the mind does not
know the difference between reality and something
strongly visualized and imagined. This is the basis for
"Picturing your way to success." What you picture in your
mind you will have happen, because your mind will perceive it as real. When you visualize a lemon strongly your
body responds as if a lemon is really there.

We used this theory to design a process to complete,
in our mind's eye, our pictures of death. This progression
process takes people forward in time to experience their
death experience. The results of these progressions have
been fascinating, and we will share some of them with
you.

One girl discovered that she had set her death event
to happen the very night that she did the progression. She
and her husband would be in an auto crash on the way
home from the Weekend. He would be driving and would
live through the accident, and she would die in the
accident. She was wearing the exact clothing that she had
on while doing the process and her lesson in this lifetime
was to heal her relationship with her husband, falling back

in love with him, and she had completed that lesson in the Weekend by falling back in love with him. She completed her death event while in the process, and before leaving the Weekend she changed her clothing, throwing away the clothes she would have been wearing to her death event. She drove home instead of him, and she drove home by a different road so as to completely avoid the circumstances of her death. Several weeks later she reviewed the progression process and there was no death event. She had completed her stand that death is inevitable.

In another case a girl had set up her death event for the next Wednesday night following the progression. She was attending the post-training meeting of a training she had completed, was wearing a red jump suit, and after that meeting she was going to be driving on the expressway in her sister's red sports car and would be in an accident with a truck, at which time she would die. She would still be wearing the name tag given to her at her meeting. Two days later she went shopping with her sister to buy an outfit to wear to the meeting, and while in the mall saw a beautiful red jump suit, just her size, and she wanted to buy it. Her sister quickly recalled the progression and reminded her that she had seen herself wearing that red jump suit when she had her death event. She was shocked to discover that she could have been wearing that outfit, so she didn't buy it. She arranged to ride with someone else to the meeting, and went by a different road, avoiding her death event. Several weeks later when she reviewed the progression process she had no death event. She had completed her stand that death is inevitable and is now physically immortal.

We are not the victims of our death, we are the source of our death, and death is the dreary back door home. We can complete our death event and our stand that death is inevitable and take the stand for physical immortality, coming alive and being safe in this world. When we are ready to go back home we can raise the vibration of our body and in a flash of light return home in a body clothed in light, a Translated Being, eternally free, "A Human Becoming God!"

We have recorded a cassette tape of the progression process to complete our death event; see the Recommended Reading List.

TRANSLATION

Given the way we have lived our life up till now, we probably would not want to live for nine hundred years. Now we can complete our past stand that death is inevitable and create a whole new possibility for being alive! This does not mean that we *have* to stay alive here for the next nine hundred years, however. When we finish our work here, we can choose to leave through the doorway called death, which is the dreary back door home, or we can choose the triumphant return home known as "Translation"! Translation is mastering the physical body and raising the vibration of our body into light, going home in a body of light, celebrating having mastered the physical.

Within our body is a mechanism that regulates the rate of vibration of our body. All matter is vibration and rest. Our vibration is regulated by our thoughts. Have you ever noticed how when you are thinking thoughts of worry, doubt, fear, or depression your body feels so heavy that you can hardly move, and when you are thinking thoughts of Love, Praise, and Gratitude your body feels much lighter? The heaviness or the lightness is caused by the rate of vibration. When we monitor our thoughts and only think the highest thoughts possible, our vibration speeds up faster and faster. In an instant we move from the physical kingdom into the spiritual kingdom in a burst of light, or become a "Translated Being," a member of the "God Kingdom"! This translation phenomenon is spoken about in the Bible with at least twelve individuals and the entire city of Enoch having gone through this triumphant return home through choice.

The translation experience is happening all around us today and is being referred to as "Spontaneous Combustion"! People who suddenly burn up in a flash of light: a girl waiting for her school bus, a man working in his garage, and so many others that the TV show *20/20* did a segment about this experience. It is possible that some of the current wave of missing children is being caused by the children Translating. Having done what they were here to do, and being complete with their lives, perhaps they are raising the vibration of their bodies and taking them with them . . . back to where they came from.

Scientists discovered this phenomenon of raising the vibration when they were trying to disguise a battleship in the early forties. The experiment used large generators to raise the vibration of the battleship to a higher frequency vibration. They hoped to create a cloud around it so it could sneak up on the enemy without being seen. They began raising the vibration higher and higher, and suddenly the battleship disappeared from view. It totally vanished from sight. It so startled the scientists that they quickly shut down the generators and soon the battleship settled back into this dimension. Many of the men on the battleship lost their sanity because they had lost control of their rate of vibration. They were coming into this dimension and going back into the spiritual dimension and they were unprepared to deal with the changes spiritually. The navy scientists quickly stopped these experiments and removed all reports on this experiment which was known as "The Philadelphia Experiment"!

We believe our purpose in this lifetime is to master the physical. All the self-help books, courses, classes, etc., are designed to assist us in mastering the physical. Our graduation when we have mastered the physical is "Translation." We have the ability to return home clothed in a body of light. We have the ability to come and go as the wind. "The last enemy that shall be destroyed is death." (I Cor. 15:26)

We feel these ideas, while new to some, are important to explore and question. Our lives are *more* than what we can see with our eyes, feel with our hands, and taste with our tongues.

You have the right to all the universe; to perfect peace, complete deliverance from sin, and to life eternal, joyous and complete in every way, as God appointed for his holy Son. T, 500

CHAPTER 14

SERVICE

When we are complete with our past, then what? Most people hang on to just a little of their past so that they have some reason to stay alive.

We believe that what we are all sent here for is to master the physical in order that we become better servants for God's message. In order to do this, we must clear away all the judgements, evaluations and stands that keep us from serving.

What most people call service is not truly service. Service is the act of selflessly giving to another or to a cause. Most people are looking for something in return for their service, some sort of acknowledgement from others or from themselves, or to be validated for being, or to have something return to them out of being in service to another. This is not service.

When you are serving others you are not even truly present. What is present is the contribution you have to make to whatever you are doing. You are not worried about how you look or how others will perceive your contribution or what is going on with yourself. You are fully present in whatever you are doing to produce the result, whether it be in love-making or at your job.

In the rare moments of true service, there is a feeling of satisfaction that just seems to happen to us, without our even trying to make it happen. When this satisfaction comes, we know that we have been of service to someone or something, and thus know that our lives do truly. make a difference.

All people really want to do is to serve someone or some cause. To be loyal and true to some ideal or person is the ultimate service for most. The main thought that must be managed when serving is "What's in it for me?" Nothing is in it for you. The satisfaction of knowing that your life makes a difference is enough. Knowing that this planet would not be the same without you, and that the contribution you make is appreciated by God, is all we can hope for. What more could we want?

Whenever you are feeling down or blue, go and serve someone, your kids, your spouse, your church or wherever you feel you can make the most difference. It will force you to stop thinking depressing thoughts and give you the opportunity to see that your life does make a difference.

When we are complete with our past, all that is left to do is to serve others in completing theirs and in acknowledging the divine beings that we all are on this planet.

Through doing God's work and serving others, we become closer to God in our hearts, minds and souls until there is nothing left for us to do but serve some more. When we serve God we can know that we will be taken care of for all eternity. This brings a feeling of "having come home," where peace and joy abide. We see people through our clarity about the divine beings that we all are. We begin interacting with them as the divine beings they are.

When we can acknowledge ourselves and others and treat our planet like the paradise that it is, we can stop destroying ourselves and live life like it was meant to be ... in Love, Praise, and Gratitude for All Things.

It will be given you to see your
brother's worth when all you want
for him is peace. And what you want
for him you will receive.   T, 405

CHAPTER 15

ALL IN THE NAME OF LOVE

Throughout this book, we have been revealing the truth about our lives. We have seen how we are one hundred percent responsible for all of the events that have happened to us in our lives. There is no one to blame for the way things have been, the way people have treated us, and the way we have treated others in our lives. The truth is we have hurt all of the people who have loved us. We have never been fully responsible for the devastation that we have been to them. When we reached our pattern in our cycle, we killed off the person we were in relationship with, just the way we did to our parents when we were young. Our heart was closed down and nothing they did would be all right with us, no matter how hard they tried to love us. We just turned them into a frog. After shutting down on them, we then took off and found the next one to repeat the pattern and cycle. We have not been nice to the people we were in relationship with. We were always justified and self-righteous about how they were the problem. The one constant in all of our previous relationships is that we were the one who was present, even though the names and faces of our lovers changed.

What keeps us stuck in this ongoing racket is that our heart is shut down. We do not experience the pain that we have caused our loved ones. Until now, our sadness and grief has been all about "Poor Little Itty Bitty Me!", feeling sorry for ourselves. If we had to experience the pain that we have inflicted on others each time we hurt them, we would stop hurting them the way we do.

The way to complete our patterns and to heal our relationships is to open up our hearts and feel the pain our loved ones are feeling. Then communicate to them that we know what we did to them, and that we are responsible for what happened in our relationship with them. When we own our responsibility, share in their grief, and forgive ourselves for our past, a healing takes place. We fall back in love with each other.

In experiencing the grief, we are talking about authentically feeling what they are feeling, with our heart open and vulnerable. If we are dramatizing the grief, we can demonstrate sadness and crying for days and no healing will take place, because we are only acting. It is only when we are open and vulnerable that a true healing occurs.

We know that all you really want is to have a loving relationship. We know that you want to be loved, nurtured, and taken care of by your king or queen.

A RELATIONSHIP THAT WORKS

The following qualities are present in a relationship that works:

1. Each member of the relationship surrenders to the other member of the relationship.

2. We listen to what each other says and make each other right about what is being communicated.

3. Each of us will ask for what we want and take what we get joyfully. We never ask for something that we know our partner cannot give us and we do ask for things that will make them stretch to give them to us.

4. We are always committed to our partner having what they want and what they ask us for.

5. In a situation in which we have a difference of opinion we surrender to whoever has the highest thought.

6. We keep our partner present with us even when we're not physically together. This means that we think of them and feel them present while we are apart.

7. Whenever our partner is upset we look at ourself to find out why we're having them be upset. How is it that we are responsible for having them be upset? Then we communicate together what we noticed and clean out what has been in between us.

8. We absolutely trust each other. Trust is a gift that we give and is neither earned nor deserved. So we give our trust even if in the past our partner proved to be untrustworthy.

9. When we are upset we ask our partner to tell us what they see going on with us. We then make them right about what they see. We know they are committed to us and want us to be successful.

10. We demonstrate our love for them by sending flowers, writing love notes, taking them out to special places, candlelight dinners and treat them like the King or Queen they are.

Following these suggestions has supported us in continuing to have a wonderful relationship. We continue to be more in love with each other and share the ecstasy we are with others.

THE MIRACLE WE ARE

This book is entitled "All in the Name of Love" because everything that we have done in our lives has been to give and receive love. The only problem has been that we have not opened our hearts to discover what love truly is. Most of us have felt in the past that we do not deserve to love or be loved. Now that we know that we do not know what love is, perhaps we will be motivated to do what needs to be done to fall in love with ourselves and others. Just reading this book will increase your capacity to love.

We encourage you to read this book in a responsible manner. Should you have an unresolved conflict, we invite you to participate in the Alivening Weekend, awareness trainings, or consult with other professionals in this field. THIS BOOK WORKS!

The purpose of our work is to have people discover the MIRACLE that it is to be human and to have us all start to question how we can individually express ourselves as the miracle that we are.

If we did nothing more than spend one extra hour a week taking care of ourselves, sending flowers to someone we love, playing with our children, visiting an ill friend, or cheering up the gas station attendant, our world would be a much livelier place to live.

We make the difference! Each of us, individually, do count. Each of us, individually, are responsible for the quality of our lives. Happiness begins in the heart and in the home. Treat yourselves with dignity, respect and honor, and others will respond likewise. Treat others with dignity, respect and honor, and you will respond to yourself likewise.

Acknowledge yourselves for your accomplishments, your persistence as well as your mistakes. Mistakes are made to learn from, so acknowledge your growing process and never, never give up on yourselves. Your life is a miracle . . . . Please, do not ever forget this.

Love yourself for something, one thing that you did to make this world a little brighter for someone else today, and begin to look for the positive in yourself and others. There are many good things happening today, and we are all a part of them. Let us begin focusing on the positive and letting go of the negative.

When you can do others no good, make sure you do them no harm.

To borrow from a favorite song, "Keep Smylin', keep shinin', and keep lovin'."

We are grateful for the privilege it has been to share
this work with you! It is our prayer that your reading this
book has contributed to your aliveness and a profound
shift has happened that will support you in having your
relationships be more alive and fun for you.

May God be with you and yours!

RECOMMENDED READING LIST

The following books and tapes are ones we have found to be most supportive of this work.

BOOKS

Ye Are Gods!, by Annalee Skarin. Shows that man himself creates every condition on earth, that the eternal source of power is released within man! It proves the truth of the great scriptures that "All that the Father has is yours!"

Beyond Mortal Boundaries, by Annalee Skarin. Death is the dreary, back-door entrance into the other world. It is the servant's entrance. But there is a great front door of glory for those who overcome!

Sons of God, by Christine Mercie. Her experience of being with Annalee Skarin, a prelude to reading *Ye Are Gods!*

The Door of Everything, by Nelson. A delightful book about the road to Immortality!

The Prosperity Secret of the Ages, by Catherine Ponder. How to channel a golden river of riches into your life. All of her books are excellent.

Rebirthing: The Science of Enjoying All of Your Life, by Leonard and Laut. The most recent and powerful book sharing about Rebirthing and the impact it can have in our lives.

Money is my Friend, by Phil Laut. A money seminar sharing new age ideas and methods to have a shift in your money consciousness.

Rebirthing in the New Age, by Leonard Orr and Sandra Ray. The first book about Rebirthing and the development of it by Leonard Orr and the people he worked with in the first years of the process.

The Secret Life of the Unborn Child, by Verny and Kelly. How you can prepare your unborn baby for a happy healthy life.

The Healing Power of Birth, by Rima Beth Star. Rima shares her experiences of underwater birth, an alternative birthing method.

Life and Teachings of the Masters of the Far East, by Baird T. Spalding. A five volume set, sharing about the lives of the masters who live in India and the miracles they are.

A Course in Miracles, Foundation for Inner Peace. A three volume set including a text book a work book and a teachers manual. This set shows us who we are and leads us towards Immortality.

Sayings from A Course in Miracles, by Varley and Fisher Tyler. "Dessert" cards which serve as uplifting thoughts to use throughout the day.

Physical Immortality, by Leonard Orr. Leonard's experience of being with the Indian Master "Babaji."

The Greatest Miracle in the World, by Og Mandino. An amazing narrative that will hold you spellbound as it reveals exciting new secrets for your personal happiness and success.

The Choice, by Og Mandino. Explores what lies behind the door of fame, success and wealth.

Sai Baba: Invitation to Glory, by Murphet. Introducing Sai Baba from India and his teachings.

Purpose: A Little Gift in the Adventure of Life!, by Buddy Sears. A refreshing look at our attributes and purpose.

Who's the Matter with Me, by Alice Steadman. A look at how our bodies respond to what we say about them in our lives.

Heal Your Body, by Louise Hayes. A fresh approach in using the power of your word to heal your body.

Jitterbug Perfume, by Tom Robbins. A novel about a couple who explore immortality.

2150 A.D., by Thea Alexander. A novel about one man's unique journey into the world of the future.

TAPES

The following tapes are used during the Alivening Weekend and may be used at your home to discover more about yourself. Most of these tapes were created by Glenn and Barbara Smyly.

Stands. This tape regresses you back to the original event at which time you took the stand about your life and allows you to re-experience and complete that event and stand!

Forgiveness, by Glenn Smyly and Rima Beth Star. Affirmations designed to complete all of the upsetting events in our lives, set to relaxing music.

Progression to Death. This tape is a progression forward in time to complete our death event so that we can be free to live as long as we choose.

Re-creating Your Ideal Birth, by Glenn Smyly and Rima Beth Star. A regression back in time to that point just prior to birth, setting the circumstances up to be how you would really like them to have been.

Past Life Recall. A regression into previous life experiences to discover some of the lessons and information that we learned being in those life times.

Money. A regression to re-experience and complete our original stand about money and then take a new stand about how money will be in our life now!

Dear Reader:

We are grateful for the privilege it has been to share this work with you. It is our prayer that your reading this book has contributed to your aliveness and a profound shift has happened that will support you in having your relationships work for you.

Please feel free to write to us and share what you have noticed about your life out of reading this book, and the differences you are aware of.

If you wish, you can order some of the books or tapes from our Recommended Reading List directly from the Alivening Project. We will ship to you via a traceable package carrier such as UPS. So, if possible, please give your street address rather than a box number. For each book or tape, add $2.50 for shipping and handling. (For addresses outside North America, please add $5 air mail for each book or tape.) In Florida, add 5% sales tax; in New Jersey, add 6%.

We can process Visa and Mastercard orders by phone (1-813-996-3659) or by mail (with your card number, expiration date, and signature). For quantity discount information, please call us.

Here is our current price list:

Books:

All in the Name of Love, Smylys 17.95

Tapes:

Stands, Smylys 15.00
Forgiveness, Smyly/Star 15.00
Progression to Death, Smylys 15.00
Recreating Your Ideal Birth, Smyly/Star 15.00
Past Life Recall, Smylys 15.00
Money, Smylys 15.00

Books:

All in the Name of Love, Smylys 17.95

Tapes:

Stands, Smylys 15.00
Forgiveness, Smyly/Star 15.00
Progression to Death, Smylys 15.00
Recreating Your Ideal Birth, Smyly/Star 15.00
Past Life Recall, Smylys 15.00
Money, Smylys 15.00

      Shipping and handling .... _____
      (For each book or tape,
      add $2.50 in North America, $5 overseas)

      Sales tax (5% Florida, 6% NJ) .... _____

    Total .... _____

Name   _____

Address   _____

City   _____ State _____ ZIP _____

Phone   _____ Country _____

    ___ Mastercard ___ Visa

Number   _____ Exp _____

Signature _____

Send orders to Alivening Publications, PO Box 1368, Land O'Lakes, FL 33539. For Visa and Mastercard orders by telephone, or for quantity discount information, call 1-813-996-3659.

    For information about the dates and locations of "Alivening Weekends" call the Alivening Center in Florida at 1-813-996-3659.